THE COST
OF BAD
BEHAVIOR

THE COST
OF BAD
BEHAVIOR

How Incivility Is
Damaging Your Business and
What to Do About It

Christine Pearson and
Christine Porath

PORTFOLIO

PORTFOLIO
Published by the Penguin Group

Penguin Group (USA) Inc., 375 Hudson Street, New York, New York 10014, U.S.A.
Penguin Group (Canada), 90 Eglinton Avenue East, Suite 700, Toronto, Ontario, Canada M4P 2Y3
(a division of Pearson Penguin Canada Inc.) • Penguin Books Ltd, 80 Strand, London WC2R 0RL,
England • Penguin Ireland, 25 St. Stephen's Green, Dublin 2, Ireland (a division of Penguin Books
Ltd) • Penguin Books Australia Ltd, 250 Camberwell Road, Camberwell, Victoria 3124,
Australia (a division of Pearson Australia Group Pty Ltd) • Penguin Books India Pvt Ltd,
11 Community Centre, Panchsheel Park, New Delhi – 110 017, India • Penguin Group (NZ),
67 Apollo Drive, Rosedale, North Shore 0632, New Zealand (a division of Pearson New Zealand
Ltd) • Penguin Books (South Africa) (Pty) Ltd, 24 Sturdee Avenue, Rosebank, Johannesburg
2196, South Africa

Penguin Books Ltd, Registered Offices:
80 Strand, London WC2R 0RL, England

First published in 2009 by Portfolio,
a member of Penguin Group (USA) Inc.

1   3   5   7   9   10   8   6   4   2

LIBRARY OF CONGRESS CATALOGING IN PUBLICATION DATA
Pearson, Christine M.
The cost of bad behavior : how incivility is damaging your business
and what to do about it / by Christine Pearson and Christine Porath.
p.   cm.
Includes bibliographical references and index.
ISBN 978-1-59184-261-3
1. Courtesy.   2. Work environment.   3. Consumer satisfaction.
I. Porath, Christine Lynne.   II. Title.
BJ1533.C9P43 2009
658.3'145—dc22   2008054662

Printed in the United States of America
Set in Fairfield Light
Designed by Helene Berinsky

To Jim Marine, my dad, with admiration, love, and gratitude
—CMP

To Mom, Dad, Michael, Carrie, and Mark
Thank you for a life full of love, support, and laughter.
—CLP

Whilst thou livest, keep a good tongue in thy head.
— WILLIAM SHAKESPEARE

FOREWORD

Little Murders

It was the first time I can remember witnessing "incivility at the work-place," though I never would have thought of it that way at the time. It was 1958 and happened in an unexpected place: the operating room at one of Boston's finest hospitals. We were a team studying doctor-nurse relationships. The surgeon was a superstar in his specialty and known to be "difficult." The duty of the OR nurse was to respond rapidly to the surgeon's requests for the use of certain devices: scalpel, knife, etc. and to anticipate what would be needed. A procedure in the OR is often tense, time-bound, pressure-filled. This was a long, grueling five-hour affair, and the surgeon became increasingly irate and rude with the nurse, feeling that she was not properly placing the instrument in his hand. He bellowed and screamed at her continually and then shouted, his face distorted with anger, "Goddamn it, nurse! *Slam* the instruments into my hand quickly and the right way!" She, in turn, complied with her own form of anger, slamming the instrument into the doctor's hand with such ferocity that by the end of the surgery, the surgeon's palms were raw and discolored.

My colleagues and I were stunned and puzzled by the whole scene and didn't know what to make of the behavior. We later wrote an article about the experience and referred to the nurse's response as "spiteful obedience."

What Christine Pearson and Christine Porath write about in this remarkable book reveals how widespread everyday incivilities are and the cost to companies and their employees. They demonstrate with a solid empirical base that one in five people in their sample claimed to be the target of incivility from a coworker at least once a week. About two-thirds told them that they saw incivility occurring among other employees no less than once a month. Ten percent said that they witnessed incivility every single day. They learned that in 2005, 95 percent of the national workforce reported experiences of incivility from coworkers. These events are more than little hurts, irritations; they're more like little deaths. In fact, the authors report that these everyday, "mundane" slights and disrespect cause stress that costs U.S. companies $300 billion a year.

And they occur daily around the world. Recently, Swedish researchers reported that workers under the yoke of bosses who were "inconsiderate, opaque, uncommunicative and poor advocates" were about 60 percent more likely to suffer from a life-threatening cardiac condition. By contrast, employees whose managers exhibited robust leadership skills were roughly 40 percent less likely to suffer from coronary events.[1] It's a global problem, the authors found, with some surprise, that 50 percent of Canadians in their study reported that they suffered incivility directly from fellow employees at least once a week. Canadians!

What struck me most about this book is the sad everydayness of incivilities. People in adjacent offices casting vacant stares. Meetings held that you should be invited to and aren't. (A thoughtful CEO told me recently that anytime you're not invited to a meeting, it's almost always a conscious decision, not simple mindlessness.) All of these hurts and bruises cause not only heartburn but also enormous stress. Equally shocking to me is our lack of conscious attention to these everyday incivilities. We let them go by unnoticed or ignored or buried somewhere where we hope it won't hurt, but it always does. Talk about the "banality of evil."

A play by Jules Feiffer, with the title I used for this foreword, opened in New York in 1967. It's about a ravaged family, the Newquists. One of the sons, Alfred, is homosexual and calls himself an "apathist," who allows himself to be beaten prostrate on a city street. He says that it's "Something I choose to happen. It is something you learn to live with."[2]

The play closed in a week. One year later the show opened in London and won the British equivalent of the Tony Award for best foreign play. In 1971, Alan Arkin made a cinematic version of the play starring Elliott Gould. This time it was a major hit in the United States, but keep in mind that the times were perilous; not only had JFK been assassinated and the Cuban Missile Crisis endangered the country but most of all, the mounting discontent with the Vietnam War showed all was not well. This serves as a reminder to all of us that a troubled world tends to incite more incivility than calmer, more peaceful, and prosperous times. Incivility around the world—I'd call it violence—tends to be heightened when the world is suffering, whether from JFK's assassination, 9/11, or the financial crisis facing us now. Which is why this book is so timely.

Every once in a while a book comes along that signals danger and promise, an axial turning point. Books like *The Greening of America, Unsafe at any Speed, Small Is Beautiful,* or *Silent Spring,* are examples. I think Pearson and Porath have written such a book, one that is thoroughly researched, clearly written, and with a set of action steps that can save lives and create workplaces that are creative and productive, humane institutions that reclaim the respect we all want and deserve.

Warren Bennis
University of Southern California

CONTENTS

PART III
The Solution

THE COST
OF BAD
BEHAVIOR

THE COST OF WORKPLACE INCIVILITY

Percentage of people in United States today who:
- Believe incivility is a problem: 80 percent
- Have experienced incivility at work: 96 percent
- Experience stress because of workplace incivility: 60 percent

Percentage of employees who:
- Believe they get *no* respect at work: 80 percent
- Claim that they are treated uncivilly at work *at least once per week*: 48 percent
- Were *dis*satisfied with the way their companies handle incivility: 3 out of 4
- Say that they would have career problems if they reported incivility: more than half
- Have reported their uncivil treatment to HR or EAP: 9 percent
- Left their jobs because they were treated uncivilly: 12 percent

Average price of replacing each of those employees: $50,000 (1.5 to 2.5 times their annual salaries)[1]

Annual cost of job stress to U.S. corporations: $300 billion[2]

Amount of time Fortune 1000 executives spend resolving employee conflicts: 7 *weeks* per year[3]

Percentage of workers treated uncivilly who:
- Get even with their offenders: 94 percent
- Get even with their organizations: 88 percent

Year in which the first publication promoting civility appeared: 1405

WORKPLACE INCIVILITY IS . . .

- Taking credit for others' efforts
- Passing blame for our own mistakes
- Checking e-mail or texting messages during a meeting
- Sending bad news through e-mail so that we don't have to face the recipient
- Talking down to others
- Not listening
- Spreading rumors about colleagues
- Setting others up for failure
- Not saying "please" or "thank you"
- Showing up late or leaving a meeting early with no explanation
- Belittling others' efforts
- Leaving snippy voice mail messages
- Forwarding others' e-mail to make them look bad
- Making demeaning or derogatory remarks to someone
- Withholding information
- Failing to return phone calls or respond to e-mail
- Leaving a mess for others to clean up
- Consistently grabbing easy tasks while leaving difficult ones for others
- Shutting someone out of a network or team
- Paying little attention or showing little interest in others' opinions
- Acting irritated when someone asks for a favor
- Avoiding someone
- Taking resources that someone else needs
- Throwing temper tantrums

INTRODUCTION

In 2003, DAVID TRUMBELL landed a challenging, well-paying job with a Fortune 500 telecommunications firm. Although the firm had interviewed many qualified candidates, Dave's enthusiasm and can-do spirit made him the company's first choice. Once he was on the job, Dave's prospects seemed bright. His new colleagues were sure that he would succeed. Less than two months later, however, he left the firm. The reason? Poor behavior—not his, but that of his new colleagues. "Leaders ran around shouting at people," Dave reported. "Employees took out their frustrations on each other. It sure wasn't what I was looking for in a job. Who treats people that way?"

American business has an incivility problem, and it's getting worse. Tune into interactions in many workplaces today and you'll spot employees speaking to subordinates in condescending tones, ignoring e-mail or phone messages, claiming excessive credit for their team's accomplishments, browsing on their iPhones or texting during meetings, and leaving malfunctioning office equipment for the next user to fix. About one-fourth of workers we polled in 1998 said they were treated rudely once or more per week; by 2005 that number had risen to nearly half. An astonishing 95 percent of workers in 2005 reported experiencing incivility from their coworkers. A recent Gallup study entitled "Feeling Good Matters in the Workplace" found that 73 percent of workers don't "feel good." Of the respondents to the Gallup poll, 14 percent say that they are actively disengaged as a result, and they admitted to doing what they can to undermine their organizations and their coworkers. The problem of incivility in the workplace has been compounded by our increasing tolerance of nasty behavior as a culture. Witness television shows like *The Sopranos*, films such as *Borat* or *Jackass*, the phenomenon of road rage, or the never-ending parade of ugly incidents at high school and sporting events.

Few business leaders take the necessary steps to stop incivility. Some don't know how to do it, and most simply don't understand how much incivility is costing them. That's where this book comes in. Drawing on a decade of pathbreaking research, *The Cost of Bad Behavior* argues that petty incidences of workplace rudeness exact a staggering economic toll that managers would be foolish to ignore.

Incivility's measurable costs alone are enormous. Job stress, for instance, costs U.S. corporations $300 billion a year[1], much of which has been shown to stem from workplace incivility. But incivility's true impact stretches far beyond that which is measurable in dollar terms. How to tally damage done by increased employee turnover, by the disruption of work teams, by the waning of helpful behavior, or by the tarnishing of corporate and individual reputations? As our research shows, incivility unleashes a set of complicated and destructive dynamics on individuals, teams, and organizations that impede performance and create organizational dysfunction on a number of levels, leading to diminished financial results. Far from a minor inconvenience to millions of American workers, workplace incivility is one of today's most substantial economic drains on American business, a largely preventable ill that begs to be addressed.

Where We're Coming From

We're not prim and proper manners crusaders. We're business school professors, one of us (Pearson) at the Thunderbird School of Global Management, the other (Porath) at the University of Southern California. We have devoted a good part of our careers to researching, writing, consulting on, and teaching about the subject.

We didn't set out to study workplace incivility. What we wanted to do, more than a decade ago, was identify workplace homicide's early warning signs. We suspected that disrespectful words and thoughtless deeds among employees bore the seeds from which violence grows. To our surprise, we found that although low-intensity bad behavior can help explain violence, it hardly ever causes it. Our hypothesis didn't pan out, but we discovered something else: that expensive but largely unseen side effects occur when one employee treats another in a disrespectful way—that is, "uncivilly."

Serious costs associated with incivility existed in virtually every organization that we studied. People who experienced incivility were affected deeply, and nearly everyone took action to get even. Targeted employees at all levels intentionally lowered their productivity, cut back work hours, lost respect for their bosses, put in minimal acceptable effort, and sometimes even left their jobs—all because of disrespectful words or deeds. Yet uncivil behavior barely registered as damaging on managers' radar. How could this be? Simple: The organizations we studied did not recognize the economic consequences of incivility, track them, or include them in accounting tallies.

What made the costs associated with incivility especially noteworthy was another finding of ours: that incivility was far more widespread than anybody had anticipated. Gathering experiences and observations from eight hundred employees in the United States, we asked them: Had incivility entered their interactions with their coworkers? The answer was a resounding yes. One in five claimed to be the target of incivility from a coworker at least once per week. About two-thirds told us that they saw incivility occurring among other employees no less than once a month. Ten percent said that they witnessed incivility among their colleagues every single day.

Initially, we wondered whether a me-first attitude on the part of some American workers might have skewed their perspectives. American workers, we thought, may have been too sensitive or demanding about their treatment at work. To test our caveat, we went on to gather views from across the border, where residents were perceived as less self-centered and better mannered. We polled 125 white-collar employees in Canada, asking them whether employee-to-employee incivilities had entered their work lives. The answer, again, was a resounding yes; in fact workplace experiences reported by Canadians were even worse than those reported in our own country. Half of the Canadians told us that they suffered incivility directly from their fellow employees at least once per week. Ninety-nine percent said that they witnessed incivility at work. One in four reported seeing incivility occurring between other colleagues every day.

If we had any lingering doubts that incivility was a widespread and tremendously costly workplace phenomenon, these were finally removed by the public response to our work. Within days of the first media reports about our research, we were swamped with phone calls, e-mail inquiries, and requests for interviews from reporters around the globe. Our findings were covered in more than 450 newspapers and magazines across the English-speaking world. Subsequent findings prompted interviews with television and radio networks in the United States, Canada, Britain, Australia, and France. We also received a flood of queries from strangers who had been targets of incivility in their own workplaces. Many told us about incidents that caused them to leave their jobs. Some still felt as if they were held hostage, unable to continue working at all. Some were relieved to learn that their strong reactions to the "little" injustices of incivility were not unique.

We didn't anticipate the breadth and depth of responses that our work had stirred, but this feedback only fueled us to dig deeper and look closer. We've since spent a decade gathering data about workplace incivility. We've interviewed employees, managers, executives, presidents, and CEOs. We've administered questionnaires, run experiments, led workshops, observed and consulted doctors, lawyers, law enforcement officers, managers, and executives as they planned for and dealt with contentious employees and clients. All told, we've gathered information from more than nine thousand people nationwide. Participants have told us about their uncivil experiences as targets, managers, leaders, witnesses, and offenders. They've described how incivility unfolds, how managers respond, how organizations react, how witnesses behave, and how targets feel. They've even shared their very valuable insights into how to curtail incivility, insights *The Cost of Bad Behavior* in turn shares with you.

This Book's Architecture

We've written *The Cost of Bad Behavior* to be concise, easy to read, and entertaining for managers and workers at all levels. We've also written it to be compelling. You'll encounter throughout a wealth of hard data drawn from our research. We will speak forthrightly, and we will speak from facts. We'll tell you all that we have learned about workplace incivility so that you can take a closer look at your own organization and your own behavior. We'll also go beyond the business world to fascinating examples of rudeness, disregard, and disrespect from popular culture and such fields as law, medicine, education, psychology, sociology, communication, marketing, and criminology.

The book is divided into three short sections. Chapters 1 through 4 introduce the phenomenon of incivility, describing its prevalence and characteristics. Chapters 5 through 11 reveal incivility's costs: whom it hurts and how. Chapters 12 through 17 describe in detail what individuals, organizations, and society as a whole can do to promote a civil environment. We've also included an Appendix for those curious about the roots of incivility. Despite their diversities of era, culture, and philosophy, historical figures as diverse as Confucius, Plato, Montezuma, and Lincoln exalted the value of civility, as you will see in the Appendix.

As readers will discover, some of these actions are easy, and all are inexpensive when compared with incivility's tremendous costs.

Nobody wins when it comes to incivility: not the firm, not the target of incivility, not even the offender. Read this book, and you'll come to appreciate the hidden toll incivility takes in terms of reduced employee performance, increased workplace stress, reduced employee retention, reduced team performance, erosion of the firm's culture, customer flight, and damage to the firm's reputation. Yet if the picture is grim, companies are by no means doomed to suffer losses from incivility. You have at hand right now the means to substantially reduce incivility and minimize its damage. What you need is the will. To that end, we hope you will come away from this book with one inescapable conclusion, both for yourself and for your organization: There are costs for bad behavior.

PART I

Incivility

1

What Is "Incivility"?

We were having our daily planning meeting, and things weren't going so well. We were off on our projected numbers, and everybody knew it. At the beginning of the meeting the manager passed out job applications for Wal-Mart. He explained that if we didn't start making our numbers immediately, several of us were going to be looking for new jobs soon. He didn't give us any tools or methods to improve; he just used intimidation to try to get us to perform better.

—Manager, Fortune 50 company

INCIVILITY IS a common complaint in today's workplace, but it hasn't always been. The concept came into vogue about a decade ago as newspapers, business magazines, and leadership groups began to explore the characteristics, causes, and consequences of bad behavior at work. Across the country, employees noticed that their colleagues were no longer behaving civilly and that something about the shift seemed to matter. A call went out for employees to behave more civilly toward one another. But what does that mean?

Our Definition

On the basis of our observations, experiences, and growing database, we (with Professor Lynne Andersson of Temple University) have defined incivility as "the exchange of seemingly inconsequential inconsiderate words and deeds that violate conventional norms of workplace conduct."[1] Let's spend some time explicating this definition.

First, incivility as we define it is not an objective phenomenon; it reflects people's subjective *interpretation* of actions and how these actions make them feel. Quite often the person interpreting actions as "uncivil" is not even the offender. Consider, for instance, the following story told by a line employee about her boss's attempt at humor: "When I was out on disability due to a severely broken ankle, my supervisor wrote an obnoxious letter about my injury. He was trying to be funny, but it was very disrespectful. I guess some people got some laughs from it, but I didn't. What made it even worse was that he circulated it to everyone, including other managers." The important point here is that the eyes of the beholder signaled humor for some, hurt for others. Sometimes the offense of incivility is intended; sometimes it is not. The incivilities listed below could be interpreted as intentionally offensive or not, depending on the participants and the context.

- Interrupting a conversation
- Talking loudly in common areas
- Arriving late
- Not introducing a newcomer
- Failing to return a phone call
- Showing little interest in another individual's opinion

A prime example of a boss whose incivility is unintentional and rooted in ignorance is Michael Scott, the infamous office manager on the hit TV show *The Office*. Almost everything Michael says is politically incorrect and uncivil. Yet he lacks emotional intelligence and fails to recognize how his actions affect his employees.

We incorporated the term "seemingly inconsequential" into our definition of incivility because we discovered that it didn't manifest the sort of blatant harmful intent that appears in incidences of workplace aggression and violence. Aggression sent victims retreating, and violence left bruises, but the residuals of incivility were subtler and, as a result, more insidious. As anyone who has worked in an office knows, incivility doesn't have to involve a lot of drama. It can occur when workers are simply disrespectful, inconsiderate, tactless, insensitive, uncaring, or rude to one another. On the television show *The Simpsons*, it's Mr. Burns's connived undercuts and Homer's clumsy prejudices. In the real world, it's the behavior of a colleague or boss who ignores another employee's contribution or makes a rude comment in a thoughtless attempt to be funny. In dramatic "real world" form, it's someone like (deceased) navy admiral Hyman G. Rickover, who bragged about shortening the front legs of his visitors' chairs so that they would squirm in his presence, or sending his plebes to isolation in his office closet so that they might "think better."[2]

If awards were given for the most outlandish workplace incivility, our nominee would be a manager described in a recent issue of *Training* magazine. During a meeting with executives, he removed his socks, asking his colleagues to smell his feet because they "smelled like strawberry shortcake."

Incivility is most subtle when it involves simple thoughtlessness or carelessness on the part of one's fellow workers. Employees at major corporations tell us about being left out of the communication loop because others thought "they couldn't handle" bad news or being kept waiting to start a meeting because "the big boss is behind schedule." We hear about decisions overruled without direct discussion or explanation, about body language and snide comments that convey disrespect and disregard. As a supervisor in a service firm told us, "Some of the hotshots around here roll their eyes when they don't agree with colleagues' views, or they turn their backs and start doing other things. They check text messages or organize their calendars while they're sitting around the table at a meeting." A manager at a production facility shared a more extreme example: "During a presentation to all of the company's international country managers and vice presidents, the division president jumped up and shouted, 'No one is interested in this stuff.'" A health care manager from the Midwest explained, "I was a new employee. I was pulling off a payroll cycle for the month of December, and I entered twelve [the calendar month] when I should have entered oh-six [the fiscal month]. The information systems supervisor called me insulting names with my new boss sitting next to me. It was my first payroll ever. As new as I was, it was an honest mistake. I was mortified. She made me feel so small." In another case, a vice president called a subordinate from her car phone asking for financial information that was not readily available. The employee did her best to provide an estimate and then promised that she could get back to the boss very quickly with a better figure. The boss replied over her speakerphone in her car full of executives that this was "kindergarten work." As the subordinate reflected, the comment made her feel "worthless" and like a "total nobody."

Should we care about even subtle forms of incivility? Most definitely! Whether or not incivility is deliberate, it remains potentially destructive because it provokes negative emotions and ensuing negative responses. Harmful effects may weigh on the target of the offense, coworkers, or teammates. Eventual costs may be borne by leaders, by the organization in which the incivility occurs, or by the offender.

Cathy, a CPA in Los Angeles, told us about her experience borrowing a book from her colleague Rick. Although he seemed reluctant when Cathy made the request, Rick did pull the book off his shelf. But as he took it down, he gave Cathy the once-over and then tagged his name prominently on the binding. "My immediate response was to reassure him," Cathy told us. "I said, 'Hey, I'll give it back, I promise.' I kind of laughed, but as soon as I turned to go back to my office, all I could think about was that he was being a total jerk and that I'd be avoiding future contact with him." Maybe Rick intended to be difficult, or maybe he just lacked the ability to monitor, evaluate, or control his own behavior. Maybe the cost to Rick was nil. But the future for smooth and easy interaction with Cathy was compromised, and there was a good chance that this seemingly inconsequential interaction would tarnish life at work for both of them.

Because incivility often seems minor, it can go completely unnoticed by everyone but the target. Offenders may not give their disregard a second thought, and when confronted, they often claim that they just can't grasp why what they did or said was "such a big deal." Even targets may wind up questioning their own perfectly understandable defensive responses. When incivility goes unnoticed, it has a tendency to spread fast, far, and wide. Using a tone that smacked of condescension, a partner in a New York law firm corrected a paralegal. Over time that became the partner's typical style of address toward the paralegal. Even though the initial arrogant comment caused the paralegal and witnesses to wriggle a bit, it did not seem that far out of line. Other attorneys who saw no organizational repercussions then started to mimic the partner's airs. After all, she was the one with the power, and employees watch their superiors to pick up behavior cues. Nobody corrected the haughty comment or even acknowledged it. Within a short time this uncivil behavior became part of the firm's culture, all because, on the surface, the negative impact seemed so inconsequential.

Power Plays

We've developed what incivility is, but we still need to explore the issue of who takes part in uncivil exchanges. When incivility occurs, one employee disregards another and the other notices. In our lingo, an *offender* treats a *target* uncivilly, and the target responds. Over the years we've learned a great deal about both of these roles. One distinction is especially noteworthy: Offenders and targets possess differing amounts of power and use this power differently.[3]

About 60 percent of the time the offender has higher job status than the target does. The harsh reality of power is that when you have it, you can abuse it and flaunt it (for a while, at least), mistreating people who don't have it. Examples of uncivil power play certainly abound in literature. In Dickens's nineteenth-century novella *A Christmas Carol*, bitter old miser Ebenezer is wretched to his subordinate, Bob Cratchit. In *Uncle Tom's Cabin*, Harriet Beecher Stowe's character Simon Legree is such a violent taskmaster that he has become a symbol of brutality toward all who lack power.

Incivility is sometimes deliberately deployed by cowardly leaders to unleash power in its most subtle form. This happens when the low-status target becomes a toady assistant who in turn commits incivility or worse on behalf of the leader. Consider how Mr. Smee responds to Captain Hook in any adaptation of J. M. Barrie's story *Peter Pan*. As boatswain of the *Jolly Roger*, Smee plays the bootlicking suck-up, willing to be kicked by Hook and to curry favor from Hook by kicking others. And then there is the character Grover Dill in the movie *A Christmas Story*. As the flunky to the bully Scut Farkus, Dill goads and harasses Ralphie at Scut's whim. Recalling his reactions to this pest, adult Ralphie describes Dill as "Scut Farkus's little toadie. Mean! Rotten!" Though these characters are fictitious, their archetype is found in many workplaces, especially those where incivility thrives. In his business classic *Management: Tasks, Responsibilities, Practices*, guru Peter Drucker warned about the wastefulness of workplace toadies who "make [their] career[s] by licking [their] boss' boots."

We should note that when incivility flows downward, offender and target needn't be in a direct reporting relationship. A more powerful offender in one department, for example, may get away with mistreating a lower-status target from another department. Whether direct or indirect, from one's own boss or someone else with greater hierarchical status, incivility can become part of a power trip. In the TV show *Scrubs*, nurses ignore residents as those residents attempt to give them orders, more seasoned residents demean their newbie colleagues, Dr. Cox humiliates senior residents, and chief of staff Dr. Kelso jerks Cox around. Incivility's twisting, turning path in this fiction comes amazingly close to some of the unpleasantries we uncover when we work with real medical professionals. In a county hospital where we conducted research, we learned how radiologists were sandwiched between a hostile union staff and a gifted but downright nasty surgeon. Staff members who were protected by their union were openly belligerent as they intentionally ignored and delayed radiologists' requests. The volatile surgeon erupted at attending radiologists whenever he felt particularly frustrated. How did the scapegoated radiologists respond? Well, they were rude to residents, who in turn mouthed off at nurses.

Recently the downward flow of anger was captured brilliantly in Lynn Johnston's comic strip *For Better or For Worse*. In the first frame Dad grumbles at Mom. Two frames later Mom takes out her anger by badgering her elder son. A couple of frames later, the elder son displaces his anger on the youngest sibling. With no one left of lesser status, the youngest sibling bashes her dolly on the floor. You can trace the same path in organizations. When anger erupts, it cascades downward as people of lesser and lesser status bear costs all the way down to the frontline workers. The problem of course is that once it hits the front line, the "dolly" they bash may be your customer.

If you're "important," you can keep other people waiting, talk in condescending tones, and demean them. As the *Toronto Star* reported, Robert Nardelli, Home Depot's former CEO, ruthlessly managed by spreadsheet with little concern for the effects of his actions. Even as Home Depot's turnover soared at all hierarchical levels, Nardelli followed up his store visits with abusive e-mails that neglected to mention any of the recipients' legitimate accomplishments.[4] In 2005, under Nardelli's "culture of fear" Home Depot took the largest drop in the American Consumer Satisfaction Index of any company in the retail sector.[5] Another notorious offender from the executive suites was Exxon's former CEO Lee Raymond. Ask a question of Mr. Raymond, and he might have brought you to tears with his nasty comments or, if he was really feeling his power, dismissed your concerns and dumped you. According to the *Washington Post*, even the board denounced Raymond's "disrespectful, rude and uneducating" treatment of shareholders.[6] The newsletter of North Star Management (a socially attuned asset management organization) was more blunt: "At his kindest, he was rude."[7]

Powerful people feel free to interrupt meetings at will, break the flow of water cooler conversations whenever they please, or chastise employees when it suits them. Some bosses will even stop meetings to embarrass their subordinates. We're reminded of an example shared by a manager from North Carolina: "My boss saw me hurriedly remove a paper clip from some documents sent to me and drop it in my wastebasket. In front of my twelve subordinates he rebuked me for being wasteful and required me to retrieve it."

When you're in control, you might even be able to throw tantrums, at least in front of people who have less power than you do. In our own careers, we've watched senior administrators duke it out in the hallways of the ivory tower, shouting accusations at one another at the tops of their lungs. Tantrums and other outrageous incivilities seem to plague the newspaper industry too. Charles "C. C." Chapin, longtime city editor of the *New York Evening World*, was notorious for these. During his tenure at the *Evening World*, Chapin fired 108 journalists. But those 108 didn't fare so badly compared with the scores who were reported to have been driven mad or to their deaths by the strains of working for him. "During the twenty years that I was city editor," boasted Chapin, "more than fifty of our staff went to their graves and nearly all of them were under forty." A reporter who called in an hour late with a story received this upbraiding from Chapin: "Your name is Smith, is it? You say you work for the *Evening World*, do you? You're a liar. Smith stopped working for the *Evening World* an hour ago."[8]

So much for incivilities stemming from abuse of power. For the remaining four times out of ten that incivility occurs in the workplace, the offender is lower than or equal to the target's hierarchical position. In fact we have found that disregard and disrespect have about equal chances (about 20 percent each) of flowing laterally across peers or upward from lower-level offenders to their higher-level targets.

When incivility flows between equals, the lack of a power difference can limit the offender's scope of action. But even those who don't outrank their targets can get away with interrupting them, at least for a while. Peers can ignore each other, and they can also strategically withhold information. A police officer in the Midwest told us that "for about two months, I made one of the other guys pretty much kiss my [expletive] before I would respond to any subsequent requests." A telecommunications designer told us that one of his colleagues avoided him at all possible times. "It severely curtailed my interest and effort at work. So what I did was take no role whatsoever in trying to head off people/ resource conflicts. I eliminated any proactive behavior . . . knowing that this colleague's success was linked to positive business results." As we've found, withholding information is common behavior and virtually risk-free because the harmful intent behind it is nearly impossible to prove.

When incivility occurs between equals, targets may also slyly sabotage their coworkers' efforts. A hospital manager in Michigan told us that he "made one of the other managers look like a fool by going to the senior VP." Respondents have also told us that they manipulate or employ gamesmanship to steal credit. "I told the instigator that I was going to tell his supervisor what happened. Then I did." Others reported "forgetting" to include a colleague as an addressee for an important e-mail notification or "blind-forwarding" the target's dumbest messages to other critics. Gossip among peers can taint their targets' reputations with well-placed morsels of fact or innuendo. As an account manager told us, "Lots of people were looking for Terry. I just told them, 'I don't know *where* he could be *this* time.' I let them draw their own conclusions."

If high-status people can flaunt their power by throwing tantrums, people who behave uncivilly to their superiors have to do it covertly. For this reason, spotting upwardly mobile rudeness requires tuning into the shadow side of organizations. Bottom-up offenders tell us that they ignore or "forget" specific details when people they dislike make requests. They also work the grapevine to their advantage, dropping a few juicy details about their superiors. Workers on loading docks have told us that they feign inefficiency so that time-sensitive shipments miss the deadline. "If it's been a good day, maybe some joking with the rest of the guys or good feedback from the boss about getting shipments out on time the day before, we'll bust it to get orders together in time for the FedEx pickup. But if it's a bad day, you could actually catch workers taking their time while they watch the clock."

Before we leave the subject of power, it's important to recognize that dimensions of personal identity beyond one's hierarchical position play a role in incivility, for both offenders and targets. Take gender. Men are about twice as likely as women to be offenders. On the other hand, when women are uncivil, they can be every bit as horrible as their male counterparts. Archetypes have been captured in books and films. Think of Cruella de Vil, or the Prada-clad devil Miranda Priestley. These characters' insensitivity to the feelings of others is mind-boggling and all too real. In the fall of 2007, *Fortune* created a blog about "crazy bosses" and heard from people who worked with their own versions of Cruella de Vil. According to one respondent, "she is a senior manager for a major business consulting firm. She has retired more careers at this firm than Social Security, including mine, because she . . . lies, distorts, manipulates, contrives, spins, et cetera to destroy anyone that may be perceived as a threat to her empire." A victim of workplace incivility herself, Lauren Weisberger, author of *The Devil Wears Prada*, is reputed to have based Miranda Priestley's character's nastiness and outlandish demands on Anna Wintour (*Vogue*'s notoriously inscrutable editor in chief) to whom Ms. Weisberger was once personal assistant.

Age also plays a role in incivility's unfolding. The fact that offenders are, on average, about half a dozen years older than their targets suggests that offenders are mindful of the target's greater vulnerability. At the extreme, you might imagine that new hires would be at greatest risk for incivility. After all, they haven't been around long enough to learn the ropes, and they probably don't have many allies yet. They'd seem to be prime targets, right? Not so. What we have found instead is that neither offender nor target tends to be a "newbie." On average, offenders are forty-one years old, while the target's average age is thirty-four. Offenders had spent about eight and a half years with their companies, but targets weren't new: They had put in a full six years.

Rude Awakenings

- Incivility is the exchange of seemingly inconsequential inconsiderate words and deeds that violate conventional norms of workplace conduct.
- A full 60 percent of incivility occurs top down, often as part of a power play.
- Upwardly aimed incivility is covert, frequently achieved through subtle sabotage.
- Men are twice as likely to be uncivil; men and women are equally likely to be treated uncivilly.
- Offenders tend to be older and more experienced than targets.

2

How Prevalent Is Incivility
in Society, Really?

> *There seems to be a rub-off effect from what goes on in schools*
> *and society. It affects organizations. It seems like people come*
> *to us with little or no sense of what's right or wrong. It's pretty*
> *tough for us to teach such fundamental values.*
>
> —Manager, info tech firm, mid-Atlantic region

WHEN A NINE-YEAR-OLD PONY League baseball player is set up to look
bad by the opposing team's adult coaches, that's incivility. When that
nine-year-old is a frail brain cancer survivor with a shunt in his head
through which he takes medication to maintain his strength, that's
newsworthy incivility. As *Sports Illustrated*, MSNBC, and ESPN.com all
reported, coaches in a Little League championship game ordered an
intentional walk so that the next player, nine-year-old cancer survivor
Romney Oaks, would make the last out of the Mueller Park Mustang
League championship game.[1] Spectators were flabbergasted, and the
actions lit a debate among politicians, sportscasters, media, and the
public about the dreadful lack of respectful behavior today.

As we look across society today, an important question for us becomes: Is incivility really as bad as it seems? The answer seems to be
yes, it's a serious problem that's getting worse. Just consider the following facts about life at school:

- In a study of 558 middle school kids in the Midwest, 446 admitted that they had been intentionally nasty to their classmates within the thirty-day period prior to the study. They teased their classmates, called them demeaning names, belittled their physical appearance, personal behaviors, family members, and friends.[2]

- Operation Respect, a nonprofit organization working to assure healthy learning environments for schoolchildren, found that 60 percent of American middle school students witness incivility at school *every single day.*[3]

- In response to a poll conducted by the National Association of Secondary School Principals, 89 percent of elementary school teachers and principals said that they face directly abusive language from students regularly.[4]

Some children are notoriously tough on each other, but educators today notice more blatant and widespread incivility at school. It's "in your face," even for teachers and principals. Our own data confirm that incivility occurs in nearly all settings today, by people of all ages, as part of their daily routines. We've already provided numbers on the prevalence of rudeness among coworkers. Ask anybody about his or her experiences as a customer, and you're likely to hear about situations in which incivility played a role. About a quarter of customers we surveyed believe disrespectful behavior from service providers is common today. The same percentage also sees it as more common than it was even as recently as five years ago. About half tell us that it's not unusual at all to see employees treat their coworkers badly, an equal amount (50 percent) reports seeing employees treat their customers badly, and about 40 percent of the customers we've surveyed tell us that they themselves experience rudeness from service employees at least once a month.[5]

Where are these uncivil encounters likely to happen? If you want to experience the richest venue for incivility, go out to break bread. Eighty percent of customers say they experience incivility in restaurants.[6] Disrespectful tone and treatment and rude, flippant comments are regular features of a bad dining experience. The waiter returns a steak that needed to be cooked a little longer, shoves it in front of your face, and adds sarcastically, "I hope *this* is good enough for you." A host tries to seat you by the busy kitchen or near the restroom even though the restaurant is nearly empty. The parking valet smiles, wishes you a pleasant dinner, and then peels out in your car.

Retail stores and government offices aren't much better. More than half of respondents claim to have uncivil experiences in these places. Customers frequently snitch on nasty providers who ignore them completely or snap at them or other customers. One woman told us of standing in line at the DMV when an employee called out the number of the next person. Thirty seconds later she called the number again. Finally, an elderly woman realized that it was her number and apologetically approached the DMV worker. Instead of showing any sort of thoughtfulness, the DMV employee chastised the customer, saying that there were many people in line and, after all, they did have a business to run. Our respondent felt that "there was no reason for the employee's reaction, except that she was clearly unhappy and had to take her anger out on someone. The customer continued to apologize, and the look on her face was just of utter shock, as if someone had never yelled at her that way. . . . Nonetheless, the DMV employee never apologized."

Nearly half the customers we surveyed experienced disrespectful behavior in airports or on airplanes. They're not alone. Negative encounters are so common that *BusinessWeek* devoted a recent cover story to "Fear and Loathing at the Airport."[7] Anxious passengers were described pushing their way to the front of the line, where they were greeted by counter agents sporting an attitude of nonchalance in telling them that their flight was running late. And it isn't just the airline staff. The *New York Times* reported a story about a Ted Airlines flight that was delayed briefly so that oxygen could be carried aboard for a passenger. When the reason for the delay was announced, some passengers became unruly. According to passenger John Paasonen, another traveler on the flight began "screaming he would miss his connection, and asking why the lady was so important."[8]

In another case, reported in the *Los Angeles Business Journal*, rudeness, annoyance, and insensitivity at an airline gate ended in physical violence and serious injury. After a two-hour delay in Newark, John Davis's twenty-three-month-old daughter wandered away from her parents and headed down a secured jetway. Davis's wife went to retrieve her but was stopped by an agent. Davis, furious that his wife had been restrained, began a confrontation that ended when he broke the gate agent's neck.[9]

Incivility in the world of air travel doesn't stop at the check-in counter or even in the terminal. Once inside the plane, passengers shove one another to claim overhead compartments and to get a jump start on deboarding. On July 29, 2007, on Continental Flight 1667 from Caracas to Newark, passengers annoyed by the flight's unscheduled diversion banged out their displeasure on the overhead storage bins.[10] The pilot radioed Baltimore, asking for assistance with the "out of control" passengers. On arrival, police took charge of unloading the passengers, filing them like criminals into a secure area until the plane was cleared for takeoff to Newark.

Many people we've interviewed shudder about incivility in health care. Ever notice patients whose obvious sense of their own importance creates an aura of incivility? They badger the receptionist, demanding to be seen . . . *now!* If the captive receptionist politely turns them away, the offenders launch into tirades about why they deserve immediate attention, despite the roomful of sorry souls who have been waiting patiently. A patient who reported such a scene to us asked, "Who do these people think they are? Apparently they're more important than all of us? How rude and selfish . . . what is it with people today?"

Unfortunately, patients aren't the only rude parties in the health care setting. More than a third of patients we surveyed claim to be fighting mad about the way they've been treated by their health care providers. The situation is so bad that some states are initiating full-blown programs for patients to register complaints. Departments or organizations in New York, Maryland, New Hampshire, Minnesota, Hawaii, Massachusetts, and Oklahoma receive and investigate patients' concerns about rudeness and a perceived lack of caring. Oklahoma's Board of Medical Licensure and Supervision reports that of the roughly 350 to 400 public complaints they receive annually, approximately half concern rudeness by the physician or his employees.[11] Such complaints are handed off to investigators, and the settlements can cost doctors and hospitals even more than those in malpractice suits.

Incivility is rocking the ivory tower too. It used to be that college teaching was a privileged profession in which teachers were respected or even revered by their students. Not anymore: More than 70 percent of respondents we surveyed think uncivil and disrespectful behavior is more common than it was five years ago. Nearly a decade ago the *Chronicle of Higher Education* ran an article entitled "Insubordination and Intimidation Signal the End of Decorum in Many Classrooms: Professors See Rise in Uncivil Behavior by Students—from Talking in Lectures to Physical Assaults."[12] Milder complaints included reading the newspaper and bringing portable televisions into class; more severe examples include insubordination and outright intimidation. At Virginia Tech, as a chemistry professor asked the class how to solve an equation, a student in the back of the class is reported to have yelled out, "Who gives a s---?" A professor we know described a similar interaction with a student who was walking out in the middle of class. When the professor asked where he was going, the student replied, "To watch a basketball game."

When it comes to grading these days, students' incivility often crosses the line and becomes outright aggression. One of our own graduate students, unhappy about his feedback on a paper, recently marched to the front of the room and announced that he would not take part in the day's team activities because he was "so furious about the comments on his paper." Another student of ours, perusing corrections to his term paper, stamped out of the classroom shouting, "What are you, some f---ing English teacher?" Then there are final course grades. We're often told by faculty colleagues that they have become afraid to give the grades that students actually deserve. And why not, when doing so can set off a minefield of nasty complaints and accusations of favoritism, sexual discrimination, and racism? Take a student at Utah State as one example. When her professor refused to elevate the final grade, the student shouted, "Well, you g-d----- bitch. I'm going to the department head, and he'll straighten you out."[13]

Incivility is also a glaring problem in the world of sports. We all have heard about the legendary incivility among hooligan soccer fans in Britain. Yet British fans are hardly exceptional. The whole "football" universe seems to be speeding in that direction. Sharp words and rude gestures from spectators and players have incited riots from Palermo to Beijing, Buenos Aires to Tehran. When the incivility spirals to aggression, those in harm's way have been pummeled and trampled to death. A little dispute plus a lot of emotion led to an international incident recently when, according to the *Toronto Star*, Chilean President Michelle Bachelet officially denounced the "unjustified aggression" by local police.[14] The matter at issue? A minor shouting match between a Chilean player and a Canadian fan.

Uncivil outbursts are legion in American sports. Consider a recent Pacers-Pistons game at which food and drinks, insults and punches flew through the stands.[15] Then there's the incident of Charles Barkley flinging the sweat he wiped off his head at an opposing team's fan. But that's minor compared to other pro athletes like Isaiah Rider, who spit on opposing fans. Or how about NBA bad boy Ron Artest, who has charged into the stands to settle a score with an uncivil fan? Uncivil fans may cross the line when they toss beer and paper cups at players. But how about a few years ago when the U.S. national soccer team played Honduras at Robert F. Kennedy Stadium? American spectators at that game showed their "spirit" (and their inclination to let rudeness rise to aggression) not only by shouting obscenities at linesmen but also by throwing bottles and flares that just missed players.[16]

Sure, you say, emotions run high when you're rooting for the home team. Maybe things get a little out of hand once in a while, but what's the harm? Well, here's the thing: Incivility can lead to shouting matches. Shouting matches can lead to occasional fistfights. And once in a while those fistfights can get brutal. Just consider the case of a Reading, Massachusetts, dad whose antics at his son's hockey game got a little out of control. His dispute with another father ended in manslaughter.[17]

Incivilities can quickly turn nasty for referees too. Within one week, sporting events at both of the top-notch high schools in Chapel Hill, North Carolina, whizzed out of control as fans and players accosted refs when the final whistle blew.[18] Verbal assaults escalated at one setting, and the ref was physically assaulted by a player at the other. Sideline rage at every level has become so prevalent that the National Association of Sports Officials now offers assault insurance to members.

There can be humor in disrespectful behavior, if you're not on the receiving end. Many a sitcom is punctuated by uncivil encounters. Take the classic Seinfeld conversation with a telemarketer. "I'm sorry," Seinfeld tells the caller, "I'm a little tied up now. Give me your number and I'll call you back later. What's that? Oh, you don't like being called at home? Well, now you know how I feel." Or how about the classic *Frasier* episode in which patrons repeatedly (and uncivilly) squeeze the brothers out of vacated tables at the Café Nervosa? Like a loser in a game of musical chairs, mild-mannered Frasier finally snaps. The scene's humor is punctuated by Frasier's admonition as he boldly (and now aggressively!) tosses the obnoxious customer out the door, saying, "Perhaps what you need is an etiquette lesson!"

We can't write about the prevalence of incivility without mentioning the invasion of cell phones. Many of us share the bewilderment: What are people thinking when they unload the intimate details of their lives on everyone in hearing range? What is so important that people must maintain phone contact in the most inappropriate of settings?

Everybody has a favorite story about cell phone incivility. Ours is that of Joseph Lancaster (not his real name, for reasons that will soon be apparent), a distinguished M.D. who attends church regularly. He can always be found seated in the last pew, near the doors. Maybe he thinks he'll be unobtrusive there, or maybe the location seems most convenient just in case he needs to rush out for a medical emergency. The problem is that while mass is being spoken, Dr. Lancaster talks (full volume!) on his cell phone without ever leaving his pew. He barks orders to his staff as the priest offers blessings and the choir sings hymns, and he does this every Sunday. Some parishioners glare at the doctor. Some seated in front of him even turn around to express their dismay. Some point to the doors or make waving hand signals to get him to leave. But Dr. Lancaster just keeps on talking, loudly, even during the most sacred holiday services.

Before we leave the world of high-tech incivility, we have to mention computer spam. For many of us, inquiries and solicitations outnumber legitimate messages. According to Wikipedia, 100 billion spams clog cyberspace *every day* (as of 2008). Despite corporate firewalls and focused e-mail lists, by the time you make your way through all the junk that accumulates, you may be on the brink of firing off your own rude responses to people posing legitimate requests.

There should be little doubt that incivility has become a plague. It touches society across contexts, jumping boundaries like brush fires. You're offended by someone on the way to work and displace it by abruptly interrupting your assistant. An uncivil meeting in the morning sets you sniping at your waiter at lunch. What are the implications of such widespread incivility? For many people, the little rudenesses and gestures of disrespect that they encounter daily are so common as to go unnoticed. Yet incivility in the workplace is noteworthy (and book-worthy!) because of the enormous, unrecorded costs borne by organizations and their members. These costs hurt the economy and society as a whole. You'll find a preview of these organizational costs in the next chapter.

Rude Awakenings

- Across contexts, incivility is pervasive and growing.
- A quarter of our respondents believe incivility from service providers is common today. The same percentage also sees it as more common than it was five years ago.
- Half the workers we've polled tell us that it's not unusual at all to see employees treat their coworkers badly.

3

What Could Incivility Cost a Company? A Case Study

A mule will labor ten years willingly and patiently for you, for the privilege of kicking you once.

—William Faulkner

IF INCIVILITY is far more prevalent in the workplace than managers and executives think, what's the harm? Or, in business terms, what's the cost? Most of us have experienced the negative effects of incivility first-hand; in this chapter, we're going to give you a sneak preview of some of the financial benefits a real firm, Cisco Systems, has realized by cultivating civility. Cisco provides a case study on the cost of bad behavior and just how and why it pays to be civil.

Founded in San Jose, California, in 1984, Cisco Systems is a public, multinational corporation that designs and sells communications and networking technology. With 2007 revenues exceeding $34 billion, Cisco attributes its success to a positive environment that enables employees to work at their best. To reinforce this positive environment, Cisco developed in 2007 a comprehensive plan to assure respectful interactions among all employees. The basis for this plan was a detailed calculation of incivility's costs, which in turn was grounded in hard data from our study of 775 non-Cisco employees who had experienced workplace incivility. We found that:

- Fifty-three percent of employees surveyed lost work time worrying about the incident and future interactions with the offender.
- Twenty-eight percent lost work time trying to avoid the offender.
- Thirty-seven percent reported a weakened sense of commitment to their organizations.
- Twenty-two percent reduced their efforts at work.
- Ten percent decreased the amount of time they spent at work.
- Forty-six percent thought about changing their jobs—to get away from the offender.
- Twelve percent actually changed jobs.

Cisco's first analytical step was to estimate how frequently incivility might actually occur in its organization. Managers started with the assumption that Cisco employees are generally quite civil. Interpersonal skills are vital selection criteria at Cisco, and mutual respect is reinforced through the culture. The relative lack of incivility at Cisco has been validated publicly: It consistently ranks among the elite of *Fortune*'s 100 Best Companies to Work For (number eleven nationwide in 2007). Taking this into account, managers presumed that only 1 Cisco employee in 100 would experience incivility at work in one year's time. With Cisco's population of 49,000 employees, this meant that 490 employees per year would experience workplace incivility. The managers then attached negative effects by calculating the probability of occurrence of incivility (0.01) as related to the effects of incivility.

Despite the very low likelihood of occurrence of incivility assumed by Cisco, the projected impact was considerable. Even if only 1 percent of Cisco employees experienced incivility at work, research results suggested that:

- Two hundred and sixty people would lose work time worrying about the incident and future interactions (one percent, or 490 people, who would experience incivility × 53 percent of those who actually lost time worrying when incivility had occurred in their organizations).

- One hundred eighty-two people would experience a weakened sense of commitment to Cisco (490 × 37 percent).
- Fifty-nine people would actually change jobs (490 × 12 percent).

Cisco's managers used these data to project expenses by annualizing revenue per employee. This led to an estimate of lost productivity value. At Cisco, an exceptionally civil company, the organization-wide costs for potential time lost by targets who worried about additional uncivil incidents and future interactions with offenders totaled nearly $2 *million* per year. With estimates for the costs of weakened commitment (also calculated as lost productivity value) and job changes (calculated on the basis of cost per hire) added in, the total topped $8 *million*. This sum is just a starting point; it doesn't include other common incivility outcomes, such as intentional reductions in the targets' effort or time spent at work. The figure also lacks any secondary costs that might be borne through colleagues of a target (whose own commitment or productivity might drop from witnessing or hearing about the incident or who might lose time on their own projects while filling in for the target) or by customers (whose perceptions of the company and buying inclinations might drop when they witness incivility among employees). As our research shows, those costs too are significant. Effects on colleagues and customers are just as harmful to the organization as effects on targets. Cisco included additional intangibles in its calculations and training programs. In particular, it noted that incivility can increase legal exposure, turnover and recruitment losses, and health care services (especially related to stress) as well as impact organizational culture profoundly.

The estimates here give only a very rough starting place from which to think about the costs of bad behavior. In the pages that follow, we provide basic financial worksheets so that you might do the same for your organization.

CALCULATING THE COST OF INCIVILITY IN YOUR COMPANY

On the basis of all that you know about your workplace, how likely is it that an employee in your organization will experience incivility from another employee? (a) _____

As in the Cisco example, the first step in calculating the cost of incivility is to estimate how frequently people in your organization encounter incivility. This number is a probability. If you believe your organization is an extraordinarily civil place to work, like Cisco, that number may be as small as 0.01 (meaning that you believe only 1 in 100 employees would experience incivility in any given year) or as high as 0.96 (the probability actually given by employees regarding their own organizations as measured across industries from data we've collected over the last decade). As you contemplate the probability for your own organization, it might be helpful to know that many employees who have responded to our surveys say that they experience incivility a lot more often than once per year; in fact 48 percent claim they are affected by incivility at work at least once per *week*!

We suggest that you investigate a bit before making your estimate. You might consider the following questions and suggestions to get started.

- Ask yourself how often you have seen or experienced incivility. (Remember that if you hold a position of power, you are very unlikely to witness incivility; offenders tend to be savvy about where and when they behave badly.)

- Ask yourself how often employees have complained to you about their colleagues' bad behavior or thoughtless comments. (Again, if you're in a power position, remember that bad news does not readily flow upward.)

- Ask your HR professionals how often they have heard about incivility among employees. If your organization collects 360-degree feedback, this can be an excellent source of information.

- Ask your employees. Unless you work in an unusually open and honest workplace, this is best done through anonymous data collection methods. The challenge here, of course, is that your employees must have some level of trust in the anonymity of the data collection method as well as in the future use of the data or you will not get honest responses. If there is a high level of incivility in your organization, it's going to be very difficult to collect accurate data internally.

- Ask yourself how often uncivil incidents have been documented. (Remember that very few incivilities actually attract the attention needed for documentation in most organizations.)

How many employees work for your organization? (b) _____

On the basis of your assumptions, how many employees will experience incivility per year?
(c) _____ [probability "a" × total employees "b"]

Use "c" to calculate some of the effects experienced by employees who are treated uncivilly in your organization.

The final step in calculating some of the negative organizational impact of incivility is to estimate the costs of each of these losses. They will vary by industry and by organization. For example, in some settings, the costs associated with losing and replacing an employee are estimated at approximately one and one-half times their annual salary; in other settings, that number can soar to three or four times their annual salary. At Cisco, the managers responsible for the Global Civility Program talked through their assumptions and their best estimates to arrive at consensus. To get the most reliable financial estimates, we urge you to do the same.

Table 1

HOW CISCO CALCULATED WHAT INCIVILITY MAY BE COSTING THEM

Step 1

How likely is it that an employee in your organization will experience incivility from another employee?   (a) _____

Step 2

How many employees work for your organization?   (b) _____

Step 3

On the basis of your assumptions, how many employees will experience incivility per year? (c)

(c) _____

[probability "a" × total employees "b"]

Step 4

Use "c" to calculate some of the effects experienced:

Number of employees who will lose work time worrying about the incident and future interactions with the offender: "c" × 53% = _____

Number of employees who will lose work time trying to avoid the offender: "c" × 28% = _____

Number of employees who will experience a weakened sense of organizational commitment: "c" × 37% = _____

Number of employees who will intentionally reduce their efforts at work: "c" × 22% = _____

Number of employees who will intentionally decrease the time they spend at work: "c" × 10% = _____

Number of employees who will think about changing their jobs: "c" × 46% = _____

Number of employees who will change jobs: "c" × 12% = _____

Step 5

Calculate the costs of each of these losses. To do this, you'll need:
- Hours worked annually by each employee
- Productivity as annualized revenue per employee
- The number of hours lost because of the uncivil interaction

Step 6

Add estimated costs for those who witness (or hear about) uncivil interactions, related stress or health care costs, legal costs, costs of managing incivility by human resources and other personnel, absenteeism, and replacement costs.[1]

Here is a little more detail on what you might consider (as Cisco did) for calculating dollar figures for each loss: lost time worrying about the incident and future interactions.

To arrive at their dollar figure, Cisco managers assumed:

- Total of 20 hours of lost work time per episode of incivility
- Total of 52 weeks of 40-hour weeks = 2,080 hours worked annually by each employee
- Productivity in annualized revenue per employee = X (this figure will vary according to your total revenue and your number of employees)
- X/2,080 = revenue per hour per employee
- 20 hours × revenue per hour per employee = estimated cost of time lost by one employee who worries about the aftermath of incivility that he/she has experienced

Bear in mind that the resulting figure estimates the dollar values of time lost for one direct target only. Even with their very respectful environment, Cisco managers and executives estimated that 490 employees per year would experience incivility. To obtain their organizational figure, they would have to multiply the dollar value by 490. To arrive at a reasonable estimate, you would need to calculate for the probability within your organization. If other employees had witnessed the episode, they might also lose time worrying if they'd be next, or they might lose time listening to their offended colleague's concerns or making up for their offended colleague's lost efforts. If offenders targeted more than one employee, the number would rise accordingly.

Again, this figure is only an initial rough estimate of one of the most obvious costs, negative impact attributable to worrying. It does not include additional types of effects, such as weakened commitment or reduced effort. It reflects no calculation of negative impact on customers. And keep in mind, these effects can be quite costly. Research involving eight thousand business units from thirty-six companies found that work groups with positive attitudes were 50 percent more likely to establish above-average customer loyalty and 44 percent more likely to achieve above-average profitability.[2] Finally, we're not even talking about the dollar costs related to team inefficiencies, lowered creativity, and reduced helpfulness, which are more difficult to quantify.

To give you a better sense of how quickly costs add up, we include an example in Table 2 from a health care organization with an annual gross income of $999,856,000. We acknowledge that some of the organization's costs are higher than some typical firms would encounter (e.g., high salaries in health care), but some may also be lower (e.g., time wasted or lost). The costs considered in this example included additional costs that we highlight in later chapters. There are others to consider too that have not been included in Table 2, like the costs of upsetting or losing customers.[3] As you look at the figures, we urge you to consider the following: Even if curtailing and correcting incivility would turn just a few of these obvious negative effects into a cost savings, wouldn't that help combat the costs of bad behavior?

Table 2
THE COSTS OF INCIVILITY IN ONE HEALTH CARE ORGANIZATION

Step 1	
How likely is it that an employee in your organization will experience incivility from another employee?	(a) 50% experience one episode of incivility per year

Step 2

How many employees work for your
organization?   (b) 10,000

Step 3

On the basis of your assumptions,   (c) 50% × 1 (incivility)
how many employees will experience   × 10,000 = 5,000
incivility per year?

Step 4

Use "c" to calculate some of the effects experienced:

Number of employees who will lose
work time worrying: 5,000 × 53% = **2,650**

Number of employees who will lose
work time trying to avoid the offender: 5,000 × 28% = **1,400**

Number of employees who will
experience a weakened sense of
organizational commitment: 5,000 × 37% = **1,850**

Number of employees who will
intentionally reduce their efforts at work: 5,000 × 22% = **1,100**

Number of employees who will intentionally
decrease the time they spend at work: 5,000 × 10% = **500**

Number of employees who will think
about changing their jobs: 5,000 × 46% = **2,300**

Number of employees who will change jobs: 5,000 × 12% = **600**

Step 5

Calculate the costs of each of these losses. To do this, you'll need
(or will need to approximate):

Hours worked annually by each employee   **2,080 hours annually**
                                          (40 hours × 52 weeks/
                                          year)

Productivity in annualized revenue per   **$100,000**
employee (including physicians and nurses)

Hours lost to worrying, avoiding the, **offender** reducing effort, time spent at work, and thinking about changing jobs	$100,000/2,080 = $48.07/hour/employee
The price for weakened sense of organizational commitment (Cisco calculated this as 3% of productivity value, then multiplied by 2,080 hours)	
Lose work time worrying	$2,650 \times \frac{1}{2}$ hour $\times$ $48.07 = $63,693.75
Lose work time avoiding the offender	$1,400 \times \frac{1}{2}$ hour $\times$ $48.07 = $33,649
Weakened sense of commitment	$1,850 \times$ (3% of productivity value [$48.07]) $\times$ 2,080 hours = $5,549,200.80
Intentionally reduce their efforts	$1,100 \times 10$ hours $\times$ $48.07 = $528,770
Decrease the time they spend at work	500×13 hours $\times$ $48.07 = $312,455[4]
Think about changing their jobs	$2,300 \times 2$ hours $\times$ $48.07 = $221,122
Replacement costs caused by exit (estimated)	$100,000 \times 600$ employees= $60,000,000

Step 6

Add estimated costs :	2 witnesses $\times$ 2 hours lost $\times$ $48.07 x
Average of 2 witnesses (per incivility)	5,000 = $961,400
Stress or health care costs	$1,500,000[5]
Legal costs (estimated)	$35,000
Costs of managing incivility by HR (estimated)	$262,500[6]

Absenteeism (estimated)	$1,443,600
Grand total estimated loss caused by incivility	$70,911,390.55 **per year**

Rude Awakenings

- Dollar costs of incivility *can* be calculated.
- Your own experiences, examples from employees, human resources knowledge, and data can help you hone cost estimates for your organization.
- Even rare occurrences of incivility in highly respectful workplaces can create profound associated expenses.
- Completing an incivility cost worksheet can be a useful way of roughly estimating how incivility is hurting your organization.

4

The Roots of Workplace Incivility

Any fool can criticize, condemn, and complain—and most fools do.

—Dale Carnegie

WHY DOES INCIVILITY plague the American workplace? One huge factor, we argue, is the larger context in which workplace incivility takes place. The office doesn't exist in a vacuum; it's both a product and a cause of attitudes and behavior in the larger culture. The disrespect and disregard toward others that saturate the larger culture also carry over to the workplace. But that's only part of the story. As this chapter argues, today's workplace incivility derives from certain social and economic developments that have fundamentally changed the nature of work. In a lean, mean global business environment, office life for most of us is more stressful. With productivity pressures mounting, our office relationships may grow weaker and less meaningful. For lots of people, work isn't as nurturing and emotionally satisfying as it once was, and an atmosphere poisoned by incivility is unfortunately one of the consequences.

Let's begin with the broader culture. A quick glance outside work reveals a widespread softening or even a dissolving of community and, with it, social boundaries of civility. In his book *Bowling Alone*, Robert Putnam argues that we're hopelessly short on social capital and that our disconnections are impoverishing our lives. Some scholars question whether Putnam got it right, but evidence certainly suggests that we don't know our neighbors as well as we once did, that we are not meeting in community groups, and that even among our families and friends we enjoy fewer face-to-face interactions. A new toughness, a feeling of independence, as if we don't need other people, has emerged. Unfortunately, we also believe that we don't need to be polite to those other people.

Some social critics contend that incivility has risen because of indulgent parenting.[1] According to this argument, New Age moms and dads of the seventies and eighties failed to hold the line with their Gen X kids. They taught those kids how to demand respect but not how to give it. There's some validity to this argument. Those Gen X "kids" are now in college and grad school, and as we describe in Chapter 3, we and our colleagues regularly struggle with their lack of respect.

"DON'T YOU REALIZE JASON, THAT WHEN YOU THROW FURNITURE OUT THE WINDOW AND TIE YOUR SISTER TO A TREE, YOU MAKE MOMMY AND DADDY VERY SAD?"

Other critics cite politics and the media as an explanation for incivility.[2] Despite the efforts of some senators, mayors, even world leaders to dial back the harshness, political arguments and debates have become so ferocious that it's hard to keep focus on the matters under consideration. At the Penn Conference on Civility and American Politics, the University of Pennsylvania's president summed up the state of political affairs by noting that "divisions have grown into chasms so deep that simply getting people into the same room to talk has become difficult. That kind of contentiousness prevents fruitful discourse and hurts the deliberative process."[3]

As for the media, many observers cite their tendency to magnify and sensationalize conflict and controversy.[4] Never before has the language on television and in movies been so vulgar, or the topics so lewd and rude. Offensive commentary and innuendo are the lifeblood of radio shock jocks like Howard Stern, Marconi and Tiny, Don Imus, Mancow Muller, and Opie and Anthony. And then there's Perez Hilton (aka Mario Lavandeira, Jr.), whose radio appearances and blogging are sufficiently offensive to have led to civil litigation. Turn to TV, and you can watch incivility daily on shows like *South Park*, *The Jerry Springer Show*, and MTV's *Jackass*, to cite a few. In the music world, the rap singer Eminem is just one of several artists who have built their careers on lyrics laced with homophobia, racism, and misogyny. Eminem has received an Academy Award and multiple Grammys and has sold more than 70 million albums worldwide.

The stressful nature of life today also plays a huge role. According to a recent poll by the watchdog agency Public Agenda, nearly half the people surveyed believe that "life is so hectic and people are so busy and pressed for time that they forget to be nice."[5] *Forget* to be nice? We talk about brain science in chapters ahead, but for now let's think about that claim from a commonsense perspective. What is taking place that is causing us to have to *remember* to be nice? Psychiatrist Edward Hallowell may come close to the answer in his *Harvard Business Review* article "Overloaded Circuits: Why Smart People Underperform." With so many demands on our time and attention, Hallowell argues, the excess data and information that we all must contend with gradually causes our brain to lose its capacity to be fully attentive or thoughtful about anything. "In a futile attempt to do more than is possible, the brain paradoxically reduces its ability to think clearly." Cognitive overloads may play out behaviorally as incivilities, in the form of tantrums, the passing of blame, or the ignoring or undermining of others. Overloaded circuitry, then, could explain why we increasingly have to *remember* to be nice.

It's impossible to ignore society's cultural leaning toward disrespect and disregard when we consider the causes for workplace incivility. Rudeness draws us into a downward, self-reinforcing cycle that pervades many areas of our lives. We watch people get away with rude and outrageous demands in public settings so frequently that it seems to be the norm. But again, that's only part of the story. Changes in the economy are also conspiring to make incivility much, much worse. In a globalized, rightsized, outsourced world, businesses everywhere are forced to do more with less in order to compete. Extraordinary customer demands and top-notch global innovation have led to increasingly complex products and services. Some workers are being stretched like bungee cords to accommodate the improvements. When uncivil behavior seems to be okay for these employees, why would anyone expect others to restrain themselves?

New employment norms have created fertile conditions for incivility. Relationships between employees and companies used to be based on loyalty. Many people worked for the same employers throughout their careers, and their loyalty was rewarded with job security. Those days are gone. In the 1980s the Conference Board asked managers if "employees who are loyal to the company and further its business goals deserve an assurance of continued agreement."[6] At that time, more than half agreed. When the Conference Board posed the same question to managers in the late 1990s, agreement dropped to 6 percent. According to a 2005 survey by the Center for Effective Organizations, 49 percent of Fortune 1000 companies have formally severed the loyalty tie in their employment contracts.[7] Employees are responsible for making themselves employable; their jobs will survive only so long as an employee's skills match the firm's needs. Add to this the legalities of "employment at will," and you'll find that businesses draw on their rights to terminate employees without any cause whatsoever in forty-five states.

Under the old exchange of loyalty for job security, some people had to tolerate disrespect occasionally. Today you are hard pressed to find any employees willing to do that. Growing numbers of workers (with major changes occurring among managers and professionals) are contract or contingency workers. When the contract ends, these employees move on to other settings. As skilled employees they build their own career paths and establish their relationships with employers on their own individual terms. One consequence is that employees have become more accustomed to getting what they want and more uncivil when they don't. Researchers at the University of Michigan tracked changes in employee power over a twenty-five-year period from 1977 to 2002.[8] Results showed that as the decades passed, employees believed they had more say in what they did on the job and how they would do it. Recent economic and social challenges like rising unemployment and off-shoring might have tempered employees' sentiments about independence, but on the issue of speaking up about complaints, voices are stronger, broader reaching, and cruder than ever.

Bosses bear the brunt of uncivil complaints. According to a Gallup poll of one million workers conducted in 2007, the most common reason employees leave is stressful or problematic relationships with their immediate supervisors.[9] Dissatisfied employees can quickly find thousands of sympathizers to grumble with. A Google search for "hate my boss chat rooms" revealed nearly two hundred thousand hits. There's actually a popular Web site called HateBoss.com, with blogs titled "Get this witch off my back," "Serious maladjusted human," and "Arrogant, lying, fake, perverted jerk." Bloggers criticize and slander their bosses, writing such lines as, "XX is a stupid bitch who doesn't understand anything about archives," "My boss XX at XX services is a true scumbag of a human," "XX is a pseudo-intellectual and a fraud." We're not suggesting that all the two hundred thousand hits lead to boss hater chat rooms, but there's no denying the popularity of the topic and the breadth of voice.

When workplace relationships become transactional rather than loyalty based, civility can seem like a giant waste of time. There's no need to keep the peace with coworkers, subordinates, or bosses, since everyone is in it only until a better deal comes along. Civility takes time and effort, an apparently unnecessary expenditure of resources. In our research, almost half of workers claim they have no time to be nice at work. The majority say they're overloaded at work and, like the population in general, claim this quashes their civility. Electronic communication from e-mail to texting to e-chatting plays a role by depersonalizing every encounter. Colleagues can undermine others and then not have to suffer the emotional consequences to which they might be subjected via face-to-face or voice interactions. As one itinerant info tech professional relates, "[I can] be honest, straightforward and upfront. I can say, 'Here are the facts.' I don't have to worry about politics. On the way in, I say, 'I am going to tell you exactly the way I feel about everything. You can take it or leave it.' "[10]

Demographics also play a role as a cause of workplace civility, and they will continue to do so. According to the 2000 U.S. Census, 82 million people fall into the baby boomers category. This generation, which currently holds seats of power in much of corporate America, will hit retirement age beginning in 2011. They are already being replaced by Gen Xers, a more frustrated, disenchanted, and cynical cohort and also perhaps a more uncivil one. Gen Xers will in turn be replaced by the even more ambitious and less loyal Gen Yers. Sadly, these twentysomethings seem to possess a narcissistic mind-set highly consistent with rudeness. According to research conducted by Professor Jean Twenge at San Diego State University, students today are about 30 percent more narcissistic than average students twenty-five years ago, as measured by standard personality inventories.[11] The problem is that if you're excessively focused on yourself, you're going to be that much less concerned about the effects of your behavior on others. As Generations X and Y come to dominate the workforce, we anticipate that there will be less and less "natural" inclination for mutual support among colleagues. As Twenge put it in a *Wall Street Journal* article, "Narcissists aren't good at basking in other people's glory, which makes for problematic . . . work relationships."[12]

All this spells bad news for our economy. Today less than 10 percent of American employees work in manufacturing.[13] In a service/knowledge-based economy, productivity derives from employees' skills, efforts, and initiatives. Not only do satisfied workers show up more often and on time, but they are also more effective and productive than their dissatisfied colleagues. While they're working, satisfied workers are more likely to look out for their colleagues and to do the right thing, both for colleagues and for their organizations. How employees feel about their workplace, then, matters more than ever. If workers are offended by uncivil behavior, the costs will be ever more pronounced.

As we've seen, incivility's causes in the workplace are many and varied. The incivilities that occur in society incite disregard and disrespect in the workplace, and workplace incivilities spill back over into society. It's a destructive exchange, and trends in demographics, competition, selfishness, time compression, information access, and individual stress make it that much worse. Perhaps the most curious thing of all is the delight we seem to find in incivility. As NBC's veteran sportscaster Bob Costas put it, "Incivility, boorishness and crassness are everywhere in the idiot culture we live in. And yet we celebrate all this edginess. This behavior is encouraged."[14]

What's eroded, then, are basic values. That's where this book comes in. If people are coming to their offices less and less aware of the basic rules of human conduct, and if it's beyond the scope of business to teach moral values, then there's always the appeal to self-interest. To the extent that workers of all ages learn that there are costs for bad behavior, even and especially under conditions of transactional employment, they'll be more inclined to mend their ways. Self-interest works in other areas; it's the driving force behind the free market system. As far as office behavior is concerned, it's worth a try.

Rude Awakenings

- Rudeness in our workplaces results from and causes uncivil attitudes and behavior in our larger culture.
- Demographics, politics, the media, life stresses, and having to do more with less all contribute to greater incivility.
- The replacement of loyalty-based employer/employee bonds with transactional bonds leaves more room for rudeness.
- In our service/knowledge-based economy, incivility spells disaster.

PART II

The Costs

5

What a Waste!
How Incivility Wrecks Performance

*If you drink much from a bottle marked "poison," it is almost
certain to disagree with you, sooner or later.*

—Lewis Carroll

WHEN WE BEGAN researching incivility a decade ago, we learned that
performance loss was one of incivility's most devastating costs. We also
knew that if we wanted managers and organizations to care about incivility, we needed to show them just how much it cost them. First, we
had to demonstrate that people who were treated uncivilly weren't accomplishing what they could. Second, we needed to attach dollar figures to these losses. These were challenging tasks; even today some of
incivility's most insidious effects remain unquantifiable. Yet that does
not mean we can't tell a compelling story. In this chapter, we evoke incivility's effects on performance by recounting the twists and turns that
our own research has taken over the last decade. Although a full accounting is impossible, the evidence we uncovered will surprise you
and we hope convince you to take action.

The Many Faces of Performance Loss

Our initial approach to quantifying incivility's performance costs involved first cataloging the ways in which it damaged performance and then quantifying these damages to the extent we could. We began by hypothesizing one obvious way in which incivility harmed performance: Might targets of incivility not purposely reduce performance to punish the organization?

Research by others certainly suggested as much. James Rilling, professor of anthropology, psychiatry, and behavioral sciences at Emory University, studies social interactions using an exercise called the ultimatum game. Pairs of participants are instructed to share something—often a pie. Although an easy way to assure respect and fairness would be for one person to cut the pie and the other to choose a piece, in this game the person who cuts the pie also decides which slice to keep. The hook that guarantees some fairness is that the second person can reject the slice offered, in which case neither gets any pie. Rilling's and colleagues' findings reveal that people do just that: They reject the offer if they're not treated respectfully and given a decent-size cut of the pie.[1]

In our earliest focus groups and interviews, we learned that targets of workplace incivility behaved no differently. When they were treated uncivilly, people felt so bad that they did what they could to punish the wrongdoer. Subsequent research revealed that incivility harmed performance by affecting two specific elements: motivation and ability. When treated uncivilly, people stopped performing, or they stopped performing as well as they could. Job satisfaction waned. Anger at the organization rose. The result was that people were simply not as motivated. Their performance dropped as they cut back effort, quality, and time.

Take Brendan Delaney, a manager at a regional bank. Brendan had always gotten along with his coworkers, and he was promoted twice and recognized by the bank on three separate occasions for providing superior customer service. Then his new boss, a vice president who was blazing down the fast track, refused to return his calls. On two occasions Brendan's boss exploded at him in front of subordinates. "I was hurt and angry and a little scared. At first I wanted to get even, but there was too much at stake. When he blew up again, I knew that he had crossed a line. I stayed another two years, but I never worked as hard again. I just didn't care as much."

As we observed, people who were treated uncivilly purposely punished their organizations by reducing the time they spent working. Some targets spent work time looking for other jobs or helping others do so. One executive told us that on the basis of his pay rate of eighty dollars an hour, he figured that his job search had cost his firm ninety-six hundred dollars. Unhappy flight attendants told us that they spent their flight time sitting in the back of the plane reading magazines, and disgruntled ramp workers recalled how they disappeared to sleep in the maintenance shack until the next plane arrived. Sometimes responses to incivility took the form of collaborative ploys that sabotaged the organization and its goals. Al, a project manager in a high-tech firm in Silicon Valley, told us how he and other professionals in the firm shared job openings and reviewed one another's résumés on company time. "It's a crazy form of cooperation and collegiality. We all like our jobs, and we obviously like each other, but the owners treat us like crap. They're basically nice guys, but they haven't got a clue how to manage people."

Other targets opted to check out early, cutting back time they had formerly spent helping the organization achieve its goals. Bronwyn, a consulting firm manager who had been treated uncivilly, told us how she refused to give her company one second more than her required forty hours per week. In her organization, consultants typically worked roughly sixty hours a week. At the billable rate of $200 per hour, her decision to check out resulted in a potential revenue loss of $192,000 a year for the organization ($200/hour $\times$ 20 hours/week $\times$ 48 weeks worked).

In general, performance losses resulting from lack of motivation were extremely costly. Even if they chose to stay in their jobs, targets became less loyal, cut back their effort, wasted time, and reduced hours spent at work. A senior vice president of a Fortune 50 firm captured this

impact succinctly: "Although they [targets] may not leave the organization, they can and do sit in the boat without pulling the oars . . . and
that may be worse than leaving."

It was relatively easy to tally the costs of lost motivation. Examining
the effects and costs of lost ability was more challenging. In our studies, incivility seemed to impact on people's ability to perform well because of the physical and cognitive tolls it took. The body and mind just
didn't seem to function as well when people were treated poorly. For
instance, one respondent named Katie recognized that the uncivil environment at her sports marketing firm made her head spin. She admitted that she spent far too much time and energy analyzing the situation
and what she was doing to herself by staying in it. "Distracted doesn't
begin to describe it. It consumed me. I called my family daily, relaying
the details. I was dumbfounded. I confided in friends at work who I
thought would be helpful in thinking through what was going on. I
sought anyone's counsel about what my best move would be in response
to the ridiculous events happening all around me. It sucked up my energy, and at the end of the day I had nothing left."

Why does incivility cause people to lose focus? One factor may be
the element of surprise. When incivility caught the workers we studied
by surprise, as it did in three out of four cases, workers spent considerable time and energy trying to understand the rude behavior: why it
occurred, why they were singled out for abuse, whether they responded
appropriately, and what they would do next. When offended workers
sought to get even, they wasted still more energy and time plotting their
actions. When they chose the high road, they occupied themselves with
justifying their offenders' behaviors or reassuring themselves of their
superior moral standing.

Across our studies, nearly 100 percent of respondents admitted to
analyzing the situation, thinking about whether the offender's behavior
was legitimate, and imagining the possible consequences if they retali-
ated. Many wondered if the offender's status in the organization somehow warranted the rude tone or flippant remark. Alternately, they
questioned if they had done something to deserve the treatment. Targets' minds wandered into the distant past, searching for any time they

might have failed to deliver good work or disappointed their offenders in some way.

Mark, a consultant, explained that he had spent at least a few hours of time analyzing his boss's rude remark about his last project, then wasted a solid ten hours or more of his own and his coworkers' time discussing whether this kind of remark was normal or he had somehow failed to meet expectations. Taking his concerns home, Mark used up another eight hours assessing the situation with his wife, brothers, and friends. After that, he reported, "I decided I was going to let it die. I'd take the high road . . . I wasn't going to make a fuss over it . . . it was too risky." As a result of choosing this path, though, he said he often reflects back on the remarks, losing task focus each time.

Taking Quantification Further

In an effort to understand better how pervasive performance loss was, we polled a large, diverse national sample of managers and employees. Did most targets' performances suffer in some way? Were they intentionally trying to punish the organization by reducing hours, effort, and quality? Were they wasting time and energy avoiding the offender? Were they wasting time thinking about the incident and planning how to respond? The results startled us:

- Forty-eight percent intentionally decreased work effort.
- Forty-seven percent intentionally decreased time at work.
- Thirty-eight percent intentionally decreased work quality.
- Eighty percent lost work time worrying about the incident.
- Sixty-three percent lost time avoiding the offender.
- Sixty-six percent said their performances declined.
- Seventy-eight percent said their commitment to the organization declined.

The effect of incivility on performance was even worse than we had anticipated. Incivility was spiraling, targets were suffering, organizations were losing people and profits, and managers who could do something about it didn't have a clue what was going on. We knew that our research could make a difference. We needed to help managers and organizations understand just how prevalent, important, and costly it was to overlook incivility.

Before we published our first research results, we gave a presentation at the Academy of Management, the oldest and largest scholarly management association in the world (home to more than seventeen thousand scholars and managers from 102 nations). Benjamin Haimowitz, the academy's media contact, had alerted us that the media were already revved up about our story. Within hours of arriving at our meeting, a reporter called from Australia at 5:00 A.M. to get the "scoop." We interviewed with the *Chicago Tribune* later that day, and before we left the meeting, we had spoken to members of the press from around the English-speaking world and France.

We wound up spending two entire days doing nothing but media interviews. Our e-mailboxes were swamped with messages from targets, managers, consultants, and academics who wanted to know more. The response was certainly atypical for academic work. A public relations professional at the University of North Carolina's business school told us that she had never seen anything like it in her twenty-year career. As we realized, this interest in itself offered some measure of just how important a problem incivility was for companies.

Since our primary responsibility as academics was to tell our story to other academics, we proceeded to submit articles to top research journals. Our work was accepted in the top theoretical journals, yet rejected by the top journals covering empirical research. The response was always the same: Fascinating topic, relevant to anyone who studies management or manages people, but you have collected extensive data from just one source, the target.

This criticism seemed to miss the point. Who better than the target, we wondered, to tell us about incivility? After all, these were the individuals who had actually experienced it. We were collecting their perspectives in scientifically acceptable ways, and their responses were important, even in the views of our toughest critics.

We faced at this time an additional, practical dilemma. The targets had told us consistently that they were hiding their reactions to incivility. They reported taking care to make sure that their responses were under the radar. How, then, could we collect meaningful data from their managers if their managers didn't know that the targets were slacking off or subtly sabotaging the workplace? In effect, our critics were asking for proof that our thousands of respondents weren't lying. They wanted as validation the managers' perspective on something of which, by design, the managers weren't aware. We knew that we needed additional "objective" data to win this battle.

Our subsequent experiments (with Amir Erez of the University of Florida) helped us pinpoint the root of performance losses.[2] Respondents were subjected to identical treatment in either the control group (those treated civilly) or the uncivil group; the same form of incivility was delivered in the same way, by the same person, in the same context. What we varied for each experiment were the occasions for incivility (or civility). Sometimes the experimenter was uncivil to participants for being late, sometimes a stranger treated participants rudely, and sometimes we asked participants simply to think about how they would react to various types of uncivil encounters.

In each manipulated situation, we considered the participants' actual performance, creativity, and helping behaviors. To measure performance, we asked participants to complete verbal tasks. To measure creativity, we asked participants to "brainstorm" uses for common objects and then rated the creativity and variety of their ideas. To measure helpfulness, we noted whether participants helped confederates (disguised members of the research team).

The results surprised us. Even with one-time, low-intensity incidents, participants who had been treated uncivilly were not able to concentrate as well. Concentration also suffered for participants who were asked merely to *imagine* an uncivil event. In both cases, those treated uncivilly lost task focus. Their short-term memories suffered; they recalled nearly 20 percent less. Their performances plummeted.

In our first study, in which the experimenter berated a confederate for being late, *other* participants performed 33 percent worse on the verbal tasks and came up with 39 percent fewer creative ideas. In our second study, in which a stranger encountered en route to the experiment was rude to participants, their performances were 61 percent worse on the verbal tasks, and they produced less than half as many ideas as those who had not been treated rudely.

Why would creativity be so strongly impaired? Psychologists and educators used to believe that creative thinking was spontaneous, like a bolt of insight. Today it's widely accepted that creativity requires concentration and the juggling of ideas. To be creative requires an extensive search through possibilities and then an elaboration and integration of those possibilities. Old information must be retrieved from long-term memory and then compared with new information stored only momentarily in short-term working memory. This demands mental agility, and any interference stifles the process. When incivility occurs, it seems to rob us of cognitive resources, decreasing attention and overloading working memory. We might think of the interference caused by incivility as an uninvited, unwelcome mental detour.

In both studies, participants who experienced incivility were 30 percent less creative. They produced 25 percent fewer ideas, and their ideas were less diverse. When asked what to do with a brick, for example, they'd offer logically consistent ideas like "build a house," "build a wall," "build a school," "make a sidewalk," or "build a church." Compare this with a sampling of the ideas generated by people who had not been treated uncivilly: "Sell the brick on eBay"; "use it as a goalpost for a street soccer game"; "hang it from a wall in a museum and call it abstract art"; "use it as a percussion instrument"; "grind it and use it as chalk"; "use it as a weight to work out"; and "decorate it like a pet and then give it to a kid as a present."

We also learned a lot about how incivility affects helpfulness. When people were treated uncivilly, their inclination to assist others dropped too. In the first study, in which no incivility had occurred, 90 percent of participants helped pick up something that had been intentionally dropped. But when the experimenter insulted a confederate for being late, only 35 percent offered any help. In the second study, 73 percent of those who hadn't experienced incivility volunteered to lend a hand. But when a confederate was rude to participants who were trying to find where the study was taking place, only 24 percent of those who had been treated uncivilly offered to help.

Performance Losses Multiplied

We had uncovered many organizational costs that were based in the targets' reactions, but that was just the beginning. How did incivility's effects on witnesses affect performance? To answer this question, we surveyed more than two hundred additional experienced employees. As we anticipated, incivility made witnesses angry. In fact they experienced two types of anger: a general angry mood and a personally targeted anger toward the offender. Respondents to the questionnaire told us that both types of anger took them off track. They admitted that when they saw incivility happening around them, they cut back their work efforts, let the quality of their work slide, and felt less committed toward their organization.

A manufacturing executive offered us this case in point. During a problem-solving meeting for an assembly line, the business team manager (BTM) in a very rude, cunning way put one of the supervisors on the spot for a lengthy time and insinuated he was not doing his job. The BTM asked for the supervisor's input but then ignored what he said. The BTM also spoke in a very condescending way toward the supervisor, who stopped giving input at that point. This particular supervisor had worked at the firm for twenty-five years and was the epitome of a people-focused person.

Our respondent was visibly upset by the comments of the BTM. But so were other witnesses. The next day the target called in sick and the hourly wage–earning machine operators didn't use their tacit knowledge to keep things going. In effect, productivity suffered because of the diminished loyalty and commitment the employees showed to the company on behalf of the supervisor. Although they hadn't even seen the aggression firsthand, the hourly workers still sought to retaliate against the company.

To understand why witnesses were reducing their performance, we looked at performance and creativity via the same word puzzles and brainstorming challenges we had applied to targets.[3] Those who witnessed incivility performed 20 percent worse on the word puzzles and produced nearly 30 percent fewer ideas in the brainstorming tasks. Witnesses to incivility were also less likely to help—even when the experimenter had no apparent connection to the uncivil participant. In both studies, only 25 percent of those who witnessed incivility volunteered to help, compared with 51 percent who didn't witness incivility.

With these results in mind, it was time to return to real organizations. We wanted to learn whether just being part of an uncivil environment could affect performance. Experience, observation, and common sense told us that a disrespectful, uncivil work environment would deplete people of energy and diminish their enthusiasm to learn new things. On the other hand, we believed that a respectful, civil environment would provide an atmosphere where people could thrive.

Collecting data from employees and their managers across a range of industries, we found that incivility sapped energy and shattered employees' motivation. People working in uncivil environments had difficulty learning as well as applying knowledge and skills. We compared employees working in the top and bottom 10 percent of civil and uncivil workplaces and found that those who worked in the most highly uncivil places reported having 26 percent less energy. They were 30 percent less likely to feel motivated and excited about learning new ideas and skills and 30 percent less likely to feel vital and alive. Those in highly uncivil environments were also 36 percent less satisfied with their jobs and 44 percent less committed to their organizations. Most telling of all, their managers rated them as performing 10 to 20 percent worse than others in the organization. In short, an uncivil environment shut people down and hampered their performance.

How precisely did performance suffer? People who worked in uncivil environments were less likely to be altruistic and courteous to other employees. They were less inclined to act in the company's best interests, whether by helping other employees with work-related problems, filling in for people who were sick, taking steps to prevent problems, encouraging others to do their jobs well, attending company functions, keeping up with developments in the company, or participating in company meetings. Although it's difficult to put a dollar figure on many of these behaviors, these losses are significant in any company.

Celebrity restaurateur Danny Meyer knows the damage that incivility can do, and he'll fire talent for it. Rude but gifted chefs don't last at his eleven restaurants because they set off bad vibes. In fact Meyer is convinced that customers can actually *taste* employee incivility, even when it's taking place back in the kitchen.

Take the marketing associate who decided to disconnect during her boss's sales pitch to a major client. Having dealt with his wrath for months, she and another project team member left him to squirm in front of the clients instead of contributing their knowledge in the face of tough questioning. As a result, the firm lost a deal worth hundreds of thousands of dollars. Maybe their silence didn't make the difference, but it certainly didn't help.

Some targets intentionally hold back their efforts until after they have left the organizations where they've been treated poorly. They take their ideas and resources to their next workplaces, thus damaging their initial employers. James, a salesperson, told us that when he took his biggest client with him to his next employer, it meant an immediate fifty-thousand-dollar gain for the new firm. In another case, a professor told us about waiting until she had arrived at her new school before submitting a guaranteed six-figure grant.

One More Drag on Performance

If you're really going to compute performance losses, you also need to take into account the time and focus of those involved in managing rudeness when it occurs. We were astounded by the amount of leaders' time sucked up by incivility. According to a study conducted by Accountemps and reported in *Fortune*, managers and executives of the Fortune 1000 firms spend as much as 13 percent of their total work time—*seven full weeks per year*—mending employee relationships and replacing workers who just can't or won't take it anymore. Think of it in dollars: Thirteen percent of the gross pay that goes to executives is wasted because they are managing the effects of incivility.[4]

This staggering loss was brought home to us via a story shared by Elizabeth, the director of human resources of a technology company. She had to manage the effects of rude e-mail that had been sent from a corporate vice president to an employee. "Both parties lost lots of time and energy, and both were very emotional. The employee claimed that fear was ballooning in her, and the VP was really angry about the employee's response." Over and above the losses incurred by the VP offender and the employee target, Elizabeth estimated that she had wasted more than 10 hours handling this dispute. Between the loss of the VP's time (150K/2,080 hours worked annually $\times$ 5 hours = $360), the target's time (70K/2,080 hours worked annually $\times$ 20 hours = $673) and the director's time (100K/2,080 hours worked annually $\times$ 10 hours = $480), the organization lost $1,513 calculated as straight salary just because of one uncivil e-mail message. This number does not reflect the fully loaded costs of employee time, nor does it project the loss in potential revenue. It doesn't account for losses that accrued because the target stopped doing the extras she typically did, nor does it account for future losses because the offender and target can no longer work as smoothly with each other.

Even if these costs were fully quantified, they would not approach costs that accrue in specialized environments. When hospital chiefs of staff and other senior administrators describe the time, energy, and financial impact of dealing with habitual instigators, the sum is shocking. As one of them told us, "Add up the cost of our time, as well as the time of legal counsel, the time of those who have to be interviewed (doctors and nurses who are affected by the offender or who witness the incivility), attach some salary figures, and you'll see that the costs skyrocket quickly." On the basis of dollar figures provided to us by one hospital, between the loss of the chief's time ($474,000/2,080 hours worked annually $\times$ 30 hours = $6,836), the target's time ($400,000/2,080 hours worked annually × 20 hours = $3,846), legal counsel's time ($350/hour × 40 hours = $14,000), those interviewed as part of the process (several doctors and nurses for a loss total of $1,150), the organization lost $25,832 because of one uncivil episode. And that didn't even include the costs of the consultant who was brought in to clean up the mess.

A CEO whom we interviewed while writing this book was frustrated with the time and energy sucked away managing incivility. He pleaded with us: "Hey, if you find any companies that *don't* have incivility issues, will you let me know? I want to apply for a job there."

Rude Awakenings

- Although the performance costs of incivility are difficult to quantify fully, targets of incivility harm their organizations in meaningful ways by purposely trying to exact retribution.
- Even when targets don't purposely seek revenge, incivility saps motivation and ability, two elements that contribute to performance.
- Targets of incivility are measurably less creative and less cognitively able.
- People who work in uncivil environments are proved to be quantifiably less helpful and less courteous.
- Managing the effects of incivility also costs organizations big bucks.

6

Amygdala Hijacking:
How Our Brains Respond to Incivility

You cannot make yourself feel something that you do not feel,
but you can make yourself do right in spite of your feelings.
—Pearl S. Buck

As FAR BACK as the early 1970s scholars from Harvard, Case Western Reserve, and other universities had discovered that enhancing emotional intelligence improved business measures such as organizational communication, retention, satisfaction, and productivity. Experts like Robert Rosenthal, Daniel Goleman, and Richard Boyatzis offered ways of improving emotional intelligence competencies (such as impulse control, self-awareness, and empathy) to enhance relationships, arguing that lack of emotional intelligence was sabotaging marriages, health, and careers.

Emotional intelligence is the ability to perceive, understand, and manage one's own emotions as well as to understand and respond to others' emotions. Research on emotional intelligence entered the popular domain in 1995, when Goleman, a scientific journalist with a Harvard Ph.D., published his international bestseller *Emotional Intelligence*. Goleman differentiated emotional intelligence from intellectual intelligence and championed a new way of thinking about what it means to be smart. His subsequent bestseller, *Social Intelligence*, opens with a powerful example of an American commanding officer in Iraq whose troops are surrounded by angry Muslim villagers. Speaking a different language from members of the hostile mob and wishing to prevent fear and anger from escalating, the officer orders his soldiers to get down on one knee and smile at the civilians. This story exemplifies emotional intelligence on the part of the officer because he not only read the emotion of the crowd correctly but also invented a way to communicate sympathetic emotions.

As far as incivility goes, the brain science of emotional intelligence is important because it helps explain people's responses to incivility: why our reactions can be so volatile, why we work so hard to get back at someone who treats us badly, why the sting of incivilities lasts so long, and why individuals' reactions escalate when a tit-for-tat cycle of incivility takes place. The concept of emotional intelligence brought to bear new knowledge about brain physiology, especially the role of a small, almond-shaped sector known as the amygdala. Scientists have long known that the amygdala triggers emotional responses. What one neuroscientist, Joseph LeDoux (of New York University), proposed is that the amygdala can act independently of the neocortex, effectively bypassing it for quick response. This is "amygdala hijacking": The amygdala takes over our response before we have time to reason through what is happening and how we should act. As LeDoux has noted, you needn't know exactly what something is to know that it may be dangerous.[1]

The scientific community used to believe that when danger loomed, information entered through our sensory organs and was then transmitted from the thalamus (a major sensory-coordinating area believed to send impulses to the cerebral cortex) to the neocortex (part of the cerebral cortex involved in sensory perception, conscious thought, and motor functions). In the neocortex, perceptions were sensed, meaning was attributed, and motor commands and higher reasoning took place. But LeDoux discovered a neural shortcut through the amygdala. Bypassing the neocortex, signals trigger action responses before complete sensing, meaning, and reasoning occur. Action within the amygdala primes the reception and processing of stimuli deemed emotionally relevant, thus enhancing and sharpening perception. When this time-saving path is activated, responses actually outpace decisions. This amygdala hijacking could explain physiologically the intensity and endurance of targets' responses to incivility.

Just as encountering a snake might cause an instinctual, unthinking response (adrenaline flowing, heartbeat quickening, reflex motions), so too might incivility trigger such amygdala hijacking. A nasty comment from a colleague can set off fight-or-flight responses, such as sweaty palms and a racing heartbeat. New evidence from neuroscience also shows that this hijacking can occur in individuals who merely witness events.[2] Impulsive responses to perceived danger can trounce rational thinking, energizing some targets and witnesses instantaneously to fight or flee.

Targets and witnesses who have taken part in our studies become quite emotional in reporting past encounters with incivility. They tell us that they "just wanted to get away from the guy," that they "couldn't even focus on what [the offender] was saying," that all they wanted to do was "find a way to escape." An emergency medical technician summarized his "flight" experiences and observations as follows: "Incivility has the power to intimidate people into silence. It isolates the targets and makes them feel ashamed and responsible. Angry words lead to physical avoidance." A female manager of a Wall Street investment firm articulated the "fight" response: "I made her [the offender] look like a fool by going to the senior vice president. It was a matter of survival." It seems that whether the snake is in the garden or in the next cubicle, fight-or-flight responses kick in.

If uncivil words and deeds cause amygdala hijacking, this phenomenon could also help explain the intensity and endurance of some targets' reactions. When an event sets off amygdala responses, those responses can rekindle associated emotional memories,[3] intensifying the situation at hand. This rekindling can occur subliminally as well, so that responses are set off without our awareness.[4] If an employee's cubicle is near the boss's office and she frequently witnesses her boss treating others badly, that pattern can hijack the witness's amygdala, burning a negative emotion into her brain. Every subsequent time this employee looks at the boss's door or some other subliminal cue associated with the imprinted negative scene, she could experience qualitatively similar negative emotions. If "wired" through amygdala hijackings, incivility could tap the storage bank capacities of the amygdala. The current sense of fear (or anger, or sadness) would then be compounded by the target's memory of previous emotional experiences.

Mary, a professional at the peak of her career, told us about the storage bank effects she was still experiencing: "During the first years of my career, Richie was my mentor. At the time we'd meet every week or two to talk about my progress. For even the smallest errors he berated me. Eventually the self-confidence that I had at the beginning was all but gone. I knew that Richie liked me as a person and that he actually thought I had some talent, but he treated me so badly. He would yell, sometimes even curse at me. It got so bad that I'd follow his insults by making demeaning cracks about myself too. Finally I got a big break and was offered a great job with a different company in another state. It's been more than a decade since I left, but this man still intimidates me, even when we run into each other by chance. I've turned down invitations to attend events because I'm still afraid of his outbursts. I know that his incivilities are in the past and that he has absolutely no power over me anymore, but I can't get the negative feelings out of my head."

Incivility may spark an effect similar to post-traumatic stress disorder, albeit in a less extreme way. Rather than register as a simple offense, it's likely that Richie's incivility traveled through Mary's amygdala, stirring negative emotional memories of earlier episodes when she was criticized. The negative emotions that Mary felt would have reflected not only the current criticism but also the storage bank of negative emotional memory. The negative emotional reaction would have been compounded and intensified by past criticisms retained within the amygdala. The reaction (in this case, to rude criticism) would have also occurred before Mary had a chance to evaluate consciously the provocation's actual nature and intensity.

Dr. Edward Hallowell refers to stress experiences like Mary's as brain burn. When stress triggers brain burn, a rush of emotions causes physiological responses (increased heart rate, erratic breathing) and a flooding of intense emotions. Anger, fear, and sorrow typically occur simultaneously, overwhelming the target. This leaves a scar that is not only psychological but physical. According to Hallowell, high levels of adrenaline pumped through the body under these conditions actually burn a hole in the brain, creating a permanent "tattoo." Once this occurs, the overwhelming emotions are never forgotten.[5]

Amygdala hijacking could also explain why incivility's impact lasts so long. LeDoux and others have asserted that even thinking about a previous emotional event can jog memories of associated emotions experienced in the distant past. We see evidence of this in our respondents' vivid and detailed recollections of uncivil treatment. When we use interviews and focus groups to inquire about past experiences of incivility, the reactions of some participants escalate to yelling or cursing about their offenders. Faces drop and eyes well up as respondents recollect the embarrassment or shame they felt as targets. Many respondents tell us that their emotional responses to incivility have lingered for long periods. A woman in South Carolina phoned us shortly after reading a summary of our research in her local paper. She told us that her boss had demeaned her repeatedly until she could take no more. She had quit her job. She knew her boss had been mean, but she still blamed herself for not being able "to rise to his demands." It had been six years since she quit, and she was still afraid to go back to work.

Just recently we heard from Cindy, a senior fire dispatcher with sixteen years' experience. Cindy described the intensity and endurance of the harm she experienced as a result of incivility by her supervisor, the battalion chief. Cindy and her boss had been friends for years, but he was going through some personal problems and seemed to be taking his frustrations out on everyone. A major fire broke out. No one died, and property loss was minor, but things did not go as smoothly as the chief had expected. He blamed Cindy for all sorts of things, including decisions he had made. Cindy was called in for a review a month later, during which the chief was "telling some incredibly weird, nasty, accusing things, telling me I should have known better." After the meeting Cindy went on private disability and remained on it for almost two years, diagnosed as a suicidal depressive. "I can't remember the smallest things," Cindy recalled. "I am almost housebound, going only where I feel safe. I still can't stand the sight of fire engines."

Cindy's case is extraordinary, but for many targets, memories of incivility retain astonishing potency. TV plots illustrate this effect of amygdala hijacking by evoking slights and the escalation of bitterness. Think of the *Seinfeld* episode "The Parking Space," in which George and Mike (another friend of Jerry's) argue over a parking spot. Their initial banter evolves into an argumentative standoff that lingers into the night, blocking traffic, sucking in passersby, and eventually leading to damage of one of their cars. Or remember *Seinfeld*'s "The Phone Message," in which George actually works himself into escalating intensities of rudeness, leaving nastier and nastier uncivil messages on his girlfriend's answering machine, not knowing that the reason she hasn't responded is that she's out of town and unable to pick up her messages.

If amygdala hijacking is triggered by incivility, the escalating and lingering nature of memories might also help explain why incivility spreads as easily as it does—both within the workplace and beyond it. Nearly all workers who are treated uncivilly vent their negative feelings. These feelings, enhanced and sustained by amygdala hijacking, are then mimicked by others, the mimicry subsequently infesting our own feelings. Employees may disregard their subordinates, pay no attention to their teammates' requests, and dodge discussions with their bosses. Others who witness their actions may behave in similar ways toward their subordinates, teammates, and bosses. Uncivil actions ignite negative feelings for additional employees. We know from our research that more than 25 percent of workers who are treated badly in their jobs displace their bad feelings. Most don't respond with head butts, as the French soccer player Zinédine Zidane did in the 2006 World Cup, but they yell at their kids, argue with their spouses, and ignore their neighbors, all because they've been on the receiving end of incivility at work and because the impact of incivility is intensified and prolonged by amygdala hijacking.

Think about emotional contagion that spills from the workplace to home, and Ralph Kramden in *The Honeymooners* may come quickly to mind. When his bus-driving days got the best of him or his get-rich-quick schemes failed, his wife, Alice, and his neighbor Ed Norton became his targets. Incivilities grew to insults and aspersions and even threats of violence: "Pow! Right in the kisser!" In each episode, incivility was resolved with confirmed affection in Kramden's weekly closing line to his wife: "Baby, you're the greatest." In real life, workplace incivilities displaced at home can erode bonds and even lead to domestic violence. Targets may continue the cycle, perpetuating incivility toward newer targets. The intensity can build with each affront. Whether contained in the workplace or spilled over into the home, incivility can cause a stockpiling of bad feelings that eventually overpowers anyone's capacity for emotional intelligence. By either route, brain science seems to be key in understanding why even the most civil among us have our limits.

Rude Awakenings

- Emotional ignorance can lead to incivility.
- When incivility occurs, it can trigger amygdala hijacking, setting off an unreasoned fight-or-flight response.
- Negative emotional responses can be compounded and intensified by imprecise memories of past encounters.
- For some, the memories of incivility linger for years.

7

Stress and Burnout

The arms of his chair are all ripped up and worn away. The [uncivil] environment has taken a real toll on him. People expect a lot of him and his IT [information technology] expertise. They're rude to him if he doesn't deliver immediately. He must feel beat up by the way he's been treated; at least that's what we figure by the looks of that chair. We steer clear of him. We've heard him go off on people and figure it's just a matter of time before he explodes.

—An executive at an entertainment company
talking about a burned-out colleague

ONE OF THE MOST significant ways in which incivility costs firms money is by raising stress levels. Not all stress and absenteeism are due to incivility, but the impact seems far greater than organizations know. Ignoring incivility allows the risk of stress to rise, threatening productivity and escalating health care costs, disability, and absenteeism. When leaders overlook incivility and associated stress factors, they ultimately risk losing valuable employees, and, as we argue, that's the most devastating consequence of all.

Stress's economic impact is huge and well-known. The American Institute of Stress, a nonprofit organization established by prominent physicians, health professionals, and others, reports that employee stress costs the U.S. economy $300 billion a year. Each year 365 million workdays are lost in sick time, long-term disability, and excessive job turnover caused by on-the-job stress. Around the globe, stress-related illnesses are a major financial drain on organizations, $200 billion per year for treatment alone.[1] The National Institute for Occupational Safety and Health estimates that 40 percent of the U.S. workforce is affected by stress, making it the top cause of worker disability. Workers' compensation claims for stress-related conditions are rising across the industrialized world. There are 1.5 times as many insurance claims for stress as for physical injuries.[2] Long-term disability claims based on stress, burnout, and depression are the fastest-growing category of claims in North America and Europe.[3]

Our latest research strongly confirms that the more uncivil the environment, the more stressed the employees. Looking at eight firms from diverse industries, including pharmaceuticals, health care, maritime, technology/computer services, utility, and nonprofit, we found that more than 60 percent of people who worked in highly uncivil environments experienced stress. More than 80 percent felt used up at the end of the day, and strong majorities also reported feeling emotionally exhausted, being "burned out," and having lost enthusiasm for their work.

Other experts we've talked to claim that disrespect at work is prevalent and that incivility also has strong psychological and physical effects. Psychologists Susan Folkman and the late Richard Lazarus have shown that ordinary daily hassles considerably outstrip major life stressors in causing people to feel bad and impairing social and work functioning.[4] Professor Claire Mayhew of Australia's Griffith University and her colleagues have found that in many cases the more indirect, covert incivilities (like denigration) resulted in more extensive emotional trauma and stress than did outright physical abuse.[5] Covert incivilities were also more debilitating to workers.

No matter what stressful emotion incivility induces, the fact is that the mere presence of stress wreaks havoc in the workplace. Incivility hurts. Employees experience a range of negative emotions when they're treated rudely, including anger, fear, and sadness. Our research has shown that anger and fear vary according to the power and status of the offenders and the people burned by their misbehavior. Targets with greater power tend to get angry when they're treated uncivilly; targets with less power tend to get scared. The effect of regular exposure to incivility is not status-bound; it makes everyone sad.

As the statistics suggest, one of the most costly effects of stress-fueled rudeness is its toll on workers' health. Stress is associated with fatigue, weight loss and gain, headaches, gastrointestinal illness, high blood pressure, muscle tension, and sleep disturbances. Stress is also linked to cognitive dysfunction, including reduced motivation and confidence, loss of concentration, and decreased productivity and creativity. Stress takes an emotional toll and is associated with anxiety, increased pessimism and cynicism, depression, loss of interest and pleasure in favored activities, increased irritability, tendency to perceive criticism where none is intended, tendency to withdraw from others, and increased use of alcohol or drugs.[6]

Our bodies were not designed to tolerate constant low-to-moderate stress. That's why the automatic response to stress is called fight or flight; our bodies prepare for an immediate brief altercation or escape, not a prolonged stressful encounter. In his book *Why Zebras Don't Get Ulcers*, Robert Sapolsky explains that when people live with average run-of-the-mill stressors like incivility for too long or too often, their immune systems pay the price. They experience big health problems, including cardiovascular disease, ulcers, cancer, and diabetes. Intermittent stressors, like uncivil incidents or even replaying in your head an uncivil incident, elevate glucocorticoid levels throughout the day, leading to a host of health-related problems, including increased appetite and obesity, even for those who eat sensibly and exercise. A study by the Harvard School of Public Health concluded that stressful jobs were as bad for women's health as smoking and obesity. Stress also affects the course of some types of cancer—particularly for those who hold in anger, as is often the case with low-status targets of incivility.

Stress fueled by incivility is also extremely costly because of its impact on employees' work and productivity. As stress increases, employees actually become less capable, since stress disrupts memory and hampers the processing of information. As Sapolsky explains, stress disrupts the "executive function," hindering your efforts to organize facts strategically and make sound judgments. When stress has this effect, it can lead to defective problem solving and more superficial, simplistic, unoriginal thinking. People under stress don't learn as well either.

Stressed employees tend to withdraw from their jobs, both psychologically and physically. One group of researchers has found that targets who experience greater incivility feel greater psychological and physical stress and withdraw from work by neglecting job responsibilities and specific tasks.[7] They also are more likely to think about exiting the organization. We've found, in addition, that an uncivil environment leads to greater burnout and that the importance or meaning of work then drops, along with job satisfaction and commitment. Burned-out employees invest less time and energy in their work, doing only what is absolutely necessary. They are also absent more often and do their work more ineptly.

Even for witnesses, incivility can cause stress. Many employees and managers tell us if they know that they'll hear and see incivility, even though they will not be the direct targets, they have to drag themselves into work. Michael Clark, who worked in the marketing department of a large sports management firm, complained how debilitating it was to show up at work each day. "It was almost as if I had a front-row seat to see who was going to be in the firing zone each day. I was usually on the sidelines, but it was stressful. It's no picnic to watch people get treated that way. Then I worried about what I should do. . . ." Researchers in Australia found that the impact of bullying on witnesses can be nearly as severe as that on targets.[8]

Employees who endure a toxic environment may experience personality changes. According to Swedish psychologist Heinz Leymann, they tend to become obsessive and depressed, manifesting hostile or suspicious attitudes, chronic nervousness, feelings of danger, emptiness, and hopelessness, isolation, and alienation.[9] When these changes occur, coping strategies are impaired, and a downward health spiral can en-sue. One target we worked with clearly fitted this pattern. Susan's personality and behavior became transformed because of her experiences of incivility. In her first months at a technology/computer services company, she developed a reputation for doing good work and was well liked by colleagues and the top management team. Over time, however, the firm's uncivil environment took its toll. Susan became obsessive, suspicious, irrational; fear took over. When incivility occurred, or when she even heard about the big boss berating someone for a careless mistake, Susan hid in her dark office, blinds closed. Her sweetness changed to hostility, and as her behavior became more radical, her manager's time was eaten away counseling her and colleagues who had grown afraid of her.

Susan's manager spent an average of seven hours a week for three months counseling Susan and her coworkers and discussing the situation with other managers and human resources. On the basis of his pay rate, seventy-two dollars per hour plus benefits, he figured that the time he spent managing Susan cost his firm more than ten thousand dollars. That doesn't include the business opportunities lost while Susan's manager focused on her problems or the time costs of coworkers, HR, and the other managers, which easily added forty thousand dollars or more to the total tally. Ultimately, the organization's leaders thought that they had no choice but to let Susan go. They were too nervous about what she might do to herself or others in the organization.

Susan is hardly the only example we've come across of incivility causing costly stress-related problems at work. In one technology organization, a manager's uncivil behavior led first to a string of employee absences. The offended employees claimed that they were having stress meltdowns, so their manager granted them extra weeks off to recuperate. Productivity suffered immediately. Because the incivility continued, when the offended employees returned to work, many of them quit. Ironically, some employees had spent recuperation time regurgitating and reevaluating the incivilities that had occurred. Others had simply invested the leave time into finding healthier work environments.

A senior marketing professional, Ann, had endured an uncivil environment for some time. She knew that it was causing stress-related side effects like headaches, sleeplessness, and hyperemotionality, but the final straw came when her manager belittled her in front of her coworkers. Ann finally thought seriously about the price she was paying and decided to follow her doctor's orders. She quit.

In some cases, stress that wouldn't be that harmful to one person can be absolutely devastating to another. In the movie *A League of Their Own*, Tom Hanks's character exclaims that "there's no crying in base-ball!" Yet we can't demand that everyone be thick-skinned. As research in behavioral neuroscience has found, we're all wired differently. The level of stress perceived by any one individual has little to do with strength of character and everything to do with physiological differences. Brains differ in their sensitivities to adrenaline, serotonin, and other stress modulators and neurotransmitters. Many of these differences are beyond our control.

Research has documented that for some people more than others, stress results in depression and other negative effects. One study reported in the journal *Science* identified stress-induced depression as determined largely by genetic differences.[10] The serotonin transporter (5-HTT) gene (known to play key roles in regulating arousal, mood, sleep, and cognition) moderates the influence of stressful events on depression. A person's response to threat, loss, humiliation, and defeat (all associated with incivility) is significantly affected by his or her genetic makeup.

Various factors influence how much stress incidents of incivility cause, including the predictability of the incivility, the target's sense of control, his or her learned helplessness, and biological differences. If certain individuals are typically rude, then each incivility muttered may not cause quite as much stress for some targets or witnesses. Likewise, how much control you feel you have—in responding or even just shouldering the incivility—is extraordinarily important in determining how stressful incivility is for someone. That's why stress from those with more power is so debilitating. Often the lack of control felt by a subordinate results in his or her sense of learned helplessness. Studies show that it takes surprisingly little in terms of uncontrollable unpleasantness to make some people give up and become helpless. Lab studies with animals and humans demonstrate convincingly that living beings struggle on all sorts of tasks after they have experienced stressors over which they have no control.[11] In these studies, even rats have trouble avoiding social aggression or competing with one another for food when they face uncontrollable or unpredictable stressors (such as shocks).

To dramatize just how differently incivility can stress out a person and how costly the stress can be, we close this chapter by relating the story of Matt, a salesman with a consistently uncivil boss. The regional office wasn't happy with the performance of the district in which Matt worked, so they sent in a turnaround agent, Larry, whose sole purpose was to shake things up. Larry was volatile, with a fondness for exploding in people's faces. He insulted employees, dismissed them, degraded their efforts, and blamed them for things over which they had no control—all without offering an apology. Larry was even uncivil to clients. During a visit with Matt to a client's store, Larry told the owner, "I see you're carrying on your father's tradition. This store looked like shit then. And it looks like shit in your hands."

Matt's stress skyrocketed. He wasn't always the target, but it was painful to watch teammates and clients suffer. Morale plummeted, and employees were frazzled. Finally, Matt mustered the courage to go to his corporate boss to let him know that the region's performance and future were at risk. Human resources got involved. People across the district, including Matt, were interviewed. Management must have spoken to Larry, because he asked to meet with Matt. Although Larry didn't apologize, he did admit, in reference to one of his blowups: "I used an atomic bomb when I could have used a flyswatter."

Matt knew that he had taken a risk by reporting Larry and had anxiously told his wife, "If they don't fire him, I'm done." Within weeks Matt got his answer: Larry was named district manager of the year. Three days later Matt had a heart attack. In hindsight, he recognized that he could no longer "take all the crap going on with Larry."

Rude Awakenings

- Incivility causes stress and burnout, leading to lower job satisfaction, poorer performance, and less commitment.
- When incivility increases stress, health problems become more prevalent.
- Dealing with the stress of incivility can waste a great deal of management time. Elevating health care and legal costs pack an added punch.

8

———————

Teams Pay a Price

The main ingredient of stardom is the rest of the team.

—John Wooden

THERE'S SOMETHING invigorating about a really effective team. When people work together to do their collective best, social bonds form, cooperation grows, and members actually want to help one another succeed. In great teams, synergies are discovered, and the outcome exceeds the contributions of individual members, sometimes exquisitely so. The magic of teams working well together yields advantages that organizations recognize. Twenty years ago less than a quarter of Fortune 1000 firms used self-managed teams; today fully 65 percent do.[1]

Civility plays a huge role in fostering good teamwork. In teams where mutual respect prevails, members are more comfortable sharing information freely and collaborating creatively. However, when teammates abuse and demean one another, the spirit of cooperation plummets in ways that can deplete organizational resources all the way to the bottom line. Although we are just starting to study the specific effects of mutual respect within teams, we have deep and broad experience in observing collaborative relationships. In our roles as consultants and professors we have worked with more than a thousand teams in organizations and in M.B.A. and E.M.B.A. classrooms. Members of these teams represent every industry and organizational function. We've worked with teams at the C-suite level, entry level, and every hierarchical rank in between. When we started focusing on our experiences and expertise at the team level, we imagined lots of reasons why incivility could chafe team performance. When we organized our thoughts around what makes a really effective team, one insight was clear: At the team level especially, bad behavior costs plenty.

Civility provides a foundation that facilitates any team's ability and readiness to share information and insights. Members who feel respected are happier to pitch in and help others, and their performance is better. The best teams we've known share some common approaches, regardless of their objectives or composition. Within top performing teams, members learn to share credit, information, and resources quickly and generously. Members rapidly overcome the fear that their teammates will humiliate them or use shared information against them. They also tend to give their all for the team. Individualism takes a backseat to collective objectives. Effective teams develop their own civil approaches to stay focused on their tasks, and they exert effort to maintain civility. They do not ignore signs of disrespect or disregard among team members. Rather, they learn how to disagree effectively and to attend to incivility's warning signals as soon as they arise. This may be as simple as asking a zealous team member to wait his turn to speak or as challenging as finding the common ground between two people with dissenting opinions.

When they're in their stride, top-notch teams intuitively shift between divergent approaches. They respectfully press for novelty and push members out of their "boxes" by challenging dearly held habits and assumptions. When the timing is right, effective teams know how to measure novelties against the dictates of reality, accept the right innovative ideas, and transition smoothly to new practices. All this allows them to obtain the result that is best for the group.

Exemplary among creative workplace teams may be those at IDEO, a design firm headquartered in Palo Alto, California. Here teams embrace divergence and convergence—and they are fundamentally civil. Criticism—even negative facial expressions—is discouraged, and enthusiasm and positive reinforcement are smiled on. Basic guidelines exist for creating innovative products under tight time and budget constraints while reinforcing civility. These guidelines include: (1) defer judgment ("have respect . . . otherwise you'll interrupt the flow of ideas"); (2) build on the ideas of others (because it's more productive than hogging the glory); and (3) one person at a time (so that no one's ideas are drowned out or missed). A civil approach has helped IDEO become a design powerhouse, gifted at integrating form and function in products as diverse as the Apple mouse, Nike sunglasses, the cockpit and cabin of Eclipse's very light jets, and ApproTEC Moneymaker Deep Lift Pump (an inexpensive, easily transportable, human-powered pump that allows African farmers to continue irrigating their land in the dry season).

The example of IDEO helps us understand what happens to teams when civility prevails, but what about when it is lacking? To find out, we gathered information from teams in maritime, utility, pharmaceutical, technology/computer services, nonprofit, and health care industries.[2] The lesson was simple and clear: The more uncivil the environment, the less employees feel connected to their teammates and the less energy and motivation they have to do their best work. In less civil teams, we found that trust is low. Members don't care as much about their team. They feel neither appreciated nor valued.

In follow-up studies, we discovered another important outcome: Uncivil environments stymie team productivity. When incivility is present, teammates pull back their efforts and clog the flow of information. Our research revealed that at the extreme, nearly one-fifth of all respondents actually refused to work with people who had been uncivil to them, even if they were teammates. Incivility damaged performance efficiencies too. Almost one-fourth of our respondents admitted that when they were treated uncivilly, they left tasks for their teammates to finish, and they reported that they did this purposely at least once or twice a week.

One powerfully negative effect of incivility within teams is that it decreases members' sense of so-called psychological safety, the feeling that the team environment is a safe place to take risks. When bruised by incivility, members of the team will be less comfortable and less likely to seek or accept feedback. They will quit asking for help, talking about errors, and informing one another about potential or actual problems. Offended team members stop experimenting and sharing their ideas. In some teams, these reactions can put lives at risk.

As black-box recordings reveal, lack of psychological safety can be lethal when the team in question is a flight crew. Even in the face of fatal mistakes or deadly erroneous assumptions, crew members who do not feel psychologically safe will hesitate to speak up, and their leaders who do not grant psychological safety will refuse to listen. A shocking case in point is that of Air Florida Flight 90, which plunged into the frozen Potomac on takeoff. Black-box recordings located after the catastrophe revealed that the copilot had made numerous attempts to warn the captain of impending danger. Sadly, a weak sense of psychological safety among Flight 90's crew members meant that the lack of conviction communicated by the copilot was dismissed in an offhanded way by the captain. The copilot and captain died, along with seventy-two of the other seventy-seven aboard.

When incivility diminishes psychological safety, team learning is handicapped too. Recent studies of cardiac surgical units at sixteen major medical centers revealed that teams in small cities and rural areas with relatively junior surgeons learned new, complicated procedures faster than teams in medical centers with vast resources, top-notch research facilities, and highly esteemed surgeons.[3] The crucial differentiating element that facilitated learning was psychological safety within the team. Teams that learned more quickly had developed environments characterized by mutual respect and trust. Members treated one another well. They felt comfortable with one another, offered ideas about how to do things better, experimented with novel approaches that might not work, pointed out problems, and admitted mistakes.

By contrast, our own research with medical teams has revealed some grisly examples of what can happen when team interactions are uncivil. Recently a physician in a hospital on the West Coast told us how the wrong medication had been administered to a patient because two physicians on the team refused to speak to each other. Their uncivil exchanges in the past had led them to act independently rather than as teammates. Fortunately in this case, the patient recovered despite his doctors' individualistic approaches. But in another case that we know, incivility that splintered the medical team actually led to a patient's death.

When teams push for efficiency and productivity without giving attention to how they achieve these outcomes, they tend to implode. Warning signals that we've seen are consistent and predictable: Tasks are completed and decisions are made by one or just a few members, individual gains trump collective benefits, deep-seated conflicts develop, and pretty soon members begin to resent (and avoid) team interactions. As these norms take hold, team members withdraw their individual contributions. The team's ability to coordinate complementary efforts declines. Members stop challenging one another effectively, and they lose focus on team objectives.

As part of a typical developmental cycle, all teams come up against challenges that can cause them to derail if incivility takes hold. The harmful effects of disregard and disrespect within a team can ignite at any stage. A popular management framework that has survived more than three decades of research and application can help us take a comprehensive perspective through the forming, storming, norming, and performing stages of team development.

When teams are *forming,* it's like one big honeymoon. Members are just getting acquainted, and they remain remarkably civil. As they learn and develop expectations for team behavior, they tend to "make nice" even as they size up their teammates and scrutinize the anticipated costs and benefits of team membership. In the forming stage, some members may begin to test their individual abilities to shape emergent team norms, but at this stage they generally do so with a light touch and a sense of humor. Even as disagreements arise, team members fall over one another in their attempts to defer so that they can maintain an air of mutual respect.

You can tell that a team has progressed into the *storming* stage when incivilities start to erupt. Power struggles take root, with members vying to take control and protect their roles. Individual behaviors press firmly against developing team norms as members set their relationship boundaries. During storming, such uncivil behaviors as making sarcastic comments, ignoring teammates' contributions, and hoarding credit become common. Incivilities can spew with special force as members struggle to influence team objectives and dominate standards of performance. Teams that make it through the storming stage learn how to temper their conflicts by extending mutual respect. They push and pull civilly. But if this doesn't occur, members rescind their efforts, question the value of team membership, and sabotage team goals, often for their individual benefit. When civility within the team forms insufficiently during the storming stage, the team is likely to disintegrate to nothing but a collection of individuals or a set of subgrouped coalitions.

If a team can temper its storming by acting with enough civility, it may progress to the *norming* stage. Here teams congeal and find the first opportunities to build true consensus and thrive cohesively. Teams develop authentic shared expectations, embrace team goals collectively, and effectively coordinate their approaches to how goals should be accomplished.

At the *performing* stage, teams finally achieve synchronization and synergy. Members bring out the best in each individual. Team goals are attained (and often surpassed) through sparkling collaborative efforts. Teams reap these benefits because members identify with the team and place genuine commitment in the team's objectives. There's no superficial attempt to "make nice." The civility that underscores the performing stage allows members to interact freely, contribute creatively, and take risks. Civility becomes self-reinforcing as team members in this stage convey trust in one another and the team by behaving civilly. Even if changes in the environment or team membership cause regression to earlier stages, effective performing teams often work together civilly to regain, readjust, and redevelop. In doing so, their capabilities and accomplishments soar.

In their book *Organizing Genius*, Warren Bennis and Patricia Ward Biederman track the developmental strengths and strains of six history-making teams, including Disney's Feature Animation Unit (credited with creating the 1937 Academy Award–winning *Snow White and the Seven Dwarfs* and other films); Lockheed's top secret Skunk Works (credited with the designs of the first supersonic jet fighter, the U-2, and the F-117A stealth fighter); and the Palo Alto Research Center (where the first user-friendly computer, the Xerox Alto, was developed). On the basis of their study, Bennis and Biederman conclude that the most exciting teams, the ones whose impact shakes the world, result from "a mutually respectful marriage" among members. In remarkable teams, members are granted freedom to do their absolute best, and their performance is guided by respectful leadership. As Bennis and Biederman put it, "Leaders of Great Groups who don't behave civilly put their very dreams at risk."[4]

Civility yields team payoffs in "ordinary" organizations too. Take a look at Southwest Airlines (SWA), and you'll find that teams share goals and knowledge freely and that team members pitch in enthusiastically to help one another get the work done. According to Jody Hoffer Gittell's book *The Southwest Airlines Way*, joint problem solving and shared goals produce high efficiency, quality, and satisfaction at SWA, whether measured in flight turnaround times, customer ratings, baggage-handling efficiency, or on-time arrivals. SWA employees aim to treat one another with respect—whether their job is to empty toilets or to fly the plane. Carefully observe SWA's gate operations, as we have, and you're likely to see employees gladly improvising and adapting to help one another meet performance goals. Delay your departure from the plane, and you'll probably spot flight attendants and pilots staying behind to work together, picking up trash, folding blankets, and stowing pillows to ready the plane for the next passengers. Civil teamwork pays off for SWA in low turnaround time (20 percent below industry standards), increased productivity (40 percent above industry standards), fewer customer complaints (by half), fewer lost bags (by one-third), and fewer flight delays (by 50 percent).[5]

So far we've focused on civility's benefits and incivility's costs within teams. It's important to realize that teams also pay a price when incivility originates *outside* the team. Even when the offender is not a team member, disrespect shown toward a teammate can push everyone in the team off track. Teammates can "catch" the negative emotions felt by their targeted colleagues even if they didn't share the experience or witness the incivility personally.[6]

In experiments with teams from accounting, nursing, and professional sports, researchers have found that moods felt by one team member readily transfer to other members.[7] Although we tend to think of emotions as inner states, motivated by our own personal feelings, recent research has shown that the act of mimicry actually causes the mimickers to experience the emotions that they are mimicking. A teammate's frown can make another team member frown and feel sadder. Mimicking a teammate's clenched fist can incite the feeling of anger. We have found in our research that even employees who only witness or hear about incivility may display and *feel* the same emotional responses that they are mimicking.

The negative impact doesn't stop with emotions. Contagion effects can also inhibit a team's thinking and behaviors.[8] In fact the more team members care about one another, the more incivility from without can impede the team's performance. Even after the initial emotional impact of rudeness has dissipated, teams often lose time and focus while members attempt to support the teammate who was treated poorly. Some teams burn up work time discussing the uncivil behaviors. Others spend work time strategizing about how to help the target or protect themselves should further incidents occur. These efforts sap time, energy, and creative zest from the team. And they all can occur under the radar, sucking up team resources without organizational detection.

Maria, a head nurse who faced an onslaught of incivilities from several of her hospital's doctors and administrators, provides a fairly common case in point. The effects on her team as a whole and its individual members were profound. Hers was a small, tightly knit team, and after the incivilities occurred, members spent a lot of time and emotional resources caring for her. They rallied to try to raise Maria's spirits. They worried about her. They questioned how she could remain in such a toxic situation. They strategized on how to protect her. Their concern was touching, but it also meant that the incivility that had occurred to one team member was debilitating the entire team. Eventually her team lost focus and its performance suffered. The entire team's emotional health was compromised. Maria took a leave of absence. Two nurses who had supported her also required leaves. After a while all three nurses left the organization because the incivilities made them feel so bad. The team lost valuable human resources, and its collective energies were drained.

It's not just negative feelings that can contaminate a team when incivility occurs; bad behaviors are contagious within teams too. Incivility within a team can cause norms to shift quickly as teammates mimic one another's actions. Professors Sandra Robinson (of the University of British Columbia) and Anne O'Leary-Kelly (of the University of Arkansas) tracked thirty-five teams in twenty organizations and found that if employees behaved negatively—said something hurtful, started an argument, criticized or griped with coworkers, said rude things about their boss or the organization, deliberately bent or broke a company rule, damaged company property, did something that harmed the organization or boss, or did work badly, incorrectly, or slowly on purpose—their teammates were much more likely to do the same.[9] In fact the closer the team, the more likely members were to pick up on one another's bad behaviors and negative moods, including incivility.

The spread of incivility within teams sometimes makes history. As depicted in ESPN's miniseries *The Bronx Is Burning*, on- and off-field incivilities within the 1977 New York Yankees severely eroded the baseball team's dynamics. A three-way power struggle among owner George Steinbrenner, manager Billy Martin, and superstar Reggie Jackson emerged, spawning any number of conflicts and controversies. Jackson caused enough friction among the team that members eventually refused to talk to him. Insults and incivilities escalated until Martin and Jackson had to be physically restrained from injuring each other.

As we've seen, well-functioning teams offer enormous upsides to a firm. Unfortunately, incivility easily derails these benefits. It fractures goodwill among members, destroys morale, damages psychological safety, limits innovation, and reduces productivity. Losses multiply as teammates catch the effects. Teammates are taken off track dealing with uncivil behavior and the rumblings it prompts. Wounds are inflicted that never fully heal. If incivility takes hold, the wonderful, transformational potential of a good team is sadly lost.

Rude Awakenings

- Incivility erodes conditions that lead to optimal team effectiveness, including cooperation, creativity, and information flow.
- When a team member is treated uncivilly, the team will waste time and energy.
- When individuals behave uncivilly, their teammates will often do the same.
- Negative emotions stirred by incivility can hit a team like a virus, spreading additional negative emotions and uncivil behavior.

9

When Employees Leave

[Today]—after 500 years or so—the scarcest, most valuable resource in business is no longer financial capital. It's talent.
                    —Geoffrey Colvin, senior editor at large, *Fortune*

IN EARLIER CHAPTERS we mention that more than half of all targets of incivility consider leaving, and that one in eight follows through on that thought. Doesn't sound so bad? Think again. Ruptured employment relationships are the most devastating way that incivility can impact a firm, certainly far more devastating than most managers realize. These are the most compelling evidence yet that it costs to behave badly.

One poll of nearly a thousand human resources professionals revealed that retention and hiring were their top concern, while another survey showed that 77 percent of companies believe that they don't have enough successors for their senior managers.[1] According to MetLife's annual Employee Benefits Benchmarking Report, more than half the corporate benefits specialists responding rated employee retention the most important benefits outcome.[2] Top HR executives we've talked with concur. One HR director explained that his company fell three thousand employees short of its hiring goal this year. It's a very desirable place to work (on *Fortune*'s Top 100 Places to Work); it just couldn't find the people it wanted. He articulated what all these data suggest: Organizations don't have talented employees to spare. Despite the more than one hundred thousand M.B.A.'s graduating from U.S.

business schools each year, there are too few talented leaders whose ultimate target is the C-suite. For some, the glamour is fading; the pains of scrutiny have exceeded the value of payoffs, and as we point out in Chapter Five, the rise of Generations X and Y are bringing new values and diminished loyalty to the workplace.

According to the U.S. Census Bureau and the General Accounting Office, the National Bureau of Economic Research, and the Conference Board, we're heading into a labor shortage. Some experts argue that the numbers are misleading because baby boomers won't retire as early as previous generations did; because a higher percentage of students have been pulled into the college system (so there will be plenty of college-prepped managers available); and because productivity will rise to compensate for any labor shortage that might occur. We would contend, however, that real challenges loom ahead and that there's never a good time to waste talent or lose valuable human resources. When companies overlook incivility, that's exactly what happens.

Companies that ignore incivility will lose big time as highly qualified labor becomes scarcer and scarcer. Before we get into the details of incivility-based exits, let's consider the costs of employee departures. The first thing to realize is that these costs far exceed the superficial costs of hiring replacements for the employees who leave. In addition to advertising and screening, there are orientation and training costs to include. Your company may be well aware of those costs, but have you added in the productivity lost while a replacement is being trained? How about the value of the network and relationships that the departing employee takes with him? And the fees for overtime or temporary workers who are needed to fill in the gap? How about the value of time spent by the administrator doing all the paperwork for applicants and candidates? Or the time needed to create the paper trail for the departing employees? How about the time that it takes HR specialists, the new supervisor, new peers, and others to interview, orient, and schmooze the finalists? Or the expenses that the finalists incur, like travel, hotels, meals? Then there are exit interviews for those who are going, as well as moving expenses for those who are coming. Applicants may require background checks, and this means time spent speaking with previous employers, educational institutions, and personal references. For executives, multiply some of these costs, as there will probably be at least a couple of on-site visits, including social functions and a familiarization trip for the spouse. In today's dreadful housing market, some companies even have to pick up the cost of the recruit's house in order to get him/her to move. These are only the quantifiable costs. Soft costs also accrue from a drop in morale or productivity or both when a talented colleague leaves or from the big difference in productivity between the experienced departing employee and her inexperienced replacement. Even when new employees have experience with their job responsibilities, there are many details to learn about the new company and environment. It takes time for any new employee to get up to full speed.

In their book *Investing in People*, Wayne Cascio and John Boudreau compare the turnover costs at SAS Institute—a computer programming firm in Cary, North Carolina, known for its low turnover rate—with software industry averages for computer programmers. The result is an annual opportunity savings estimate of more than $15 million per thousand programmers per year. No matter what your industry, financial effects are felt at any level when employees exit. Even for minimum wage positions, where basic reading skill is not required, turnover costs have been estimated by the Society for Human Resource Management at thirty-five hundred dollars per employee.[3] That number is about as low as exit costs get. In general, expect departures of lower-level employees to cost your organization 30 to 50 percent of their annual salaries. For middle-level employees, the cost of exit rises to an estimated 150 percent of each departing employee's yearly salary. For high-level employees, the figure can top 400 percent of their annual salary. Cascio and Boudreau note that when workers leave Merck, the firm estimates costs at 1.5 to 2.5 times the exiting employees' annual salaries. Even when young, relatively inexperienced auditors leave, we're told that Ernst and Young estimates the associated costs at 150 percent of the departing employee's salary.[4]

It's easy enough to tabulate costs for your own firm. Start with a ratio by level (as we said, 30 to 50 percent annual salary at the bottom of the pyramid, 150 percent at the middle, 400 percent at the top). Then, following Cascio and Boudreau, consider both performance and replaceability. Factor in how effective this exiting individual is and how easily he or she can be replaced. High performers who are difficult to replace are the costliest. According to *Fortune*, even in the global environment, where billions of new employees are now available from places like China and India, it's still difficult to find talented managers and professionals.[5] And incivility enters square into the middle of the talent shortage. According to one poll, the most sought-after skill in managers is the ability to motivate and engage others. Next is the ability to communicate. When incivility takes hold in an organization, it negates people's strengths and best efforts in both areas.

Conditions That Sway Targets out the Door

Targets who have been treated badly enjoy a number of options. They can quit on the spot. They can give the customary (and civil) two weeks' notice. They can keep working while looking for a better option, while trying to ignore or overcome their negative responses to the offender or trying to improve the environment and make it more civil.

Employees leave for one reason: They believe they'll be better off somewhere else. When incivility spurs departure, employees think there are more respectful organizations, places where incivility will not be condoned. A health care professional who had been with his small firm for a little over a year decided to look for a new job after his boss, a four-year veteran, belittled him for asking for follow-up clarification about concepts that had been brought up at a meeting. The target decided that he was dealing with a no-win situation and that it was better to move on. He had already watched good people leave quickly, and it was no wonder: His boss acted as though she were always 100 percent right. As he told us, "Politicians survive here. I'm not going to hang around long enough to be terminated for trumped-up reasons." He withheld information from his boss, decreased the time and effort he put in at work, and intentionally avoided his boss, but he continued working and collected full pay and benefits until he found another job.

Some people are so desperate to escape incivility that they put themselves into free fall to get away from the uncivil environment. Ryan, a director of external affairs, was appalled when his colleague in another area confided to him that he didn't "even bother to learn names anymore. People are quick to pick up on the rude environment here, and then they leave." One exceptional employee who left after being treated poorly told Ryan, "I don't care where I go. I'm leaving." She didn't have another job lined up and was afraid she'd be out of work for several months. It didn't matter; going was better than staying. Another professional gave notice shortly after joining the organization. She told Ryan that she had no other job lined up, but she wasn't going to stay in such a disrespectful place.

When jobs are plentiful and high-quality employees scarce, people are more likely to leave. They don't bother sticking around to see if they can improve things. Why put in all that effort when they can to find another job? Employees who feel connected to the organization, management, teammates, or individual coworkers are more likely to stay. The trouble is that incivility quashes feelings of connectedness. No one is drawn to people or environments that make them feel bad. We have found that people who feel sad because of incivility adopt one strategy consistently: They exit. They do so to avoid their offenders and reduce reminders and memories of the incivilities they have experienced. And since it takes determination and risk to voice dissatisfaction, employees will usually neither stay nor make the effort to improve the organization if they don't believe that their complaints will lead to positive change.

Trish described her experiences in a very large financial services company where she witnessed incivility once or twice a week and eventually became the target. Her boss, who had been with the firm a few years longer than she had, was disrespectful and dishonest. Trish thought about trying to make things better, but after talking with other managers, colleagues, friends outside work, and her manager's manager, she decided to leave. Her boss's supervisors always sided with him, even when contradictory evidence was brought forward by a group of subordinates, so what was the point of trying to fight it? Trish noticed that her boss was good at kissing up, and even when multiple employees witnessed his bad behavior, no action was taken by management. Trish cut back her efforts at work and avoided her boss as much as she could. Her commitment to the company plummeted. Eventually she changed jobs and was very glad that she did.

Employees' decisions about whether to leave or stay are usually based on their past experiences and observations of others who tried to push for improvement. In the past, when people complained about the offender or the uncivil environment, had things improved? Did management listen to complaints? Had uncivil employees been corrected? Or had people continued to get away with rudeness, despite complaints? Worse still, had offenders been perversely rewarded with promotions, plum tasks, perks, or salary increases? When complaints go unanswered, a culture of incivility can fester and spread. In our survey research, we examined how the targets' work environment related to the likelihood of exit. There's no ambiguity to the data. Where tolerance for incivility exists, employees are less satisfied and more likely to leave.

To voice their discontent, targets have to know how to do so. Some firms collect employee complaints and comments anonymously by phone or suggestion boxes; some firms use the Internet. Starbucks has a scrolling entry point on its home page where anyone can share an idea or begin an e-discussion. It also has an unusual Rumor Response page on which queries and facts about the latest buzz are shared. When such outlets don't exist, organizations lose opportunities to improve, and targets lose opportunities to vent or make suggestions for improvement. This can cause unhappy workers to leave, as Nelson did. As a seasoned new hire in the high-tech sector of the transportation industry, Nelson was frustrated that he and his new colleagues were being ignored. "We weren't learning what we needed, and then, when we had questions, people acted like we were stupid." Nelson and fellow newbies commiserated about how useless the month of training had been and how amazed they were that nobody seemed to care. Experienced workers offered no assistance. By the end of the first week on the job Nelson had had enough. Even when he quit, no one seemed to care. The company had wasted Nelson's salary for the five weeks he had been on the job. It had also wasted the trainer's salary, advertising costs, recruiting and screening expenses, and preparation of all the inital employment paperwork needed by corporate and the government. Now the firm had to start all over again by hiring new people. Two of the eight hires Nelson had trained with left within the first week, and others left eventually too. Nelson estimated that the company had wasted a hundred thousand dollars. But worse, productivity was farther behind than before Nelson and his cohort had been hired. "There was already a ridiculous backlog of work. It's all still there, and now there will be more because it takes a month of training before people can even start the job and they haven't even started advertising for replacements yet."

In another instance a managing partner of a law firm told us how another partner's uncivil behavior took a toll on the organization. Adam's incivility led to a string of turnovers among new attorneys. Within just a couple of years at least six attorneys and two paralegals left the firm because of Adam's behavior. After two years of trying to persuade him to get coaching or counseling, management added up just how much it was costing to keep him. The toll was at least $2.8 million over those two years, and the costs were still mounting.[6] Knowing the dollar figure made it easier to terminate Adam, but the partners knew that the biggest loss was the damage to the firm's reputation, which had curtailed its ability to attract and retain top attorneys. It was impossible to put a price tag on that.

Exit is particularly troublesome for organizations when it affects their best employees, those most attractive to their competitors. When the top employees leave, every departure can reduce the overall quality of the organization's employee pool. If turnover is high, firms can find themselves unable to attract or retain good employees. A downward spiral of voluntary turnover can spin a firm into decline as lesser and lesser-quality employees fill its jobs. A classic case is that of Fairchild Electronics, a semiconductor pioneer of the 1970s whose history is reported by Ed Lawler in *Treat People Right!*[7] By treating employees poorly, Fairchild lost talent to Intel and others. Not only did key staff leave, but it also became difficult for Fairchild to hire. Eventually its bad reputation did it in, and Fairchild went out of business.

When organizations ignore employees' criticisms, those who exit learn to leave in silence. The organization loses opportunities to learn, recuperate, and improve. Brad Jones was a seasoned professional who had just started as a crew scheduler at a commuter airline headquartered in the Southwest. When he was hired, he was amused that his new boss kept repeating that the job was *so* challenging and *so* stressful that people couldn't take it; new hires didn't last long, he told Brad, because the job tasks were so stressful. Brad soon learned that the stress did not come from the job tasks, as the boss assumed, but from the job environment. "Flat out," Brad told us, "it was a horrible place to work." New hires lacked passwords needed to access critical data, so they had to break from their work to ask experienced workers for their passwords several times an hour. "They actually cursed at us under their breath every time we asked," Brad explained. "It was a nightmare." The final straw came around midnight when Brad reported a scheduling problem to a senior manager who told him to call the chief pilot at home immediately. Brad reminded him that it was 3:00 A.M. on the East Coast, where the chief pilot lived, but the manager didn't care. Of course the chief pilot was furious for being disturbed in the middle of the night, and he demanded to know who had ordered the call. According to Brad, "the senior manager actually refused to give his name. What place operates like that?" Brad quit the next day. Some of the other employees in his training class had already left. Reflecting on the situation, Brad said, "I guess the guy who hired us will go on convincing himself that stressful job tasks are causing their ridiculous turnover. He just ought to take a look around at the people working for him."

Organizations face another departure cost when the direct target of incivility leaves. Acts of incivility (or reports of it that might be shared through the grapevine) can remind other employees of everything they dislike about their workplace: the boss, the hours, the job tasks, the physical environment, the equipment, even the benefits package. The target's departure can focus other employees' attention on greener pastures and better options. Many respondents describe a turning point when they realize, "If *that* guy can find a better job, I certainly can!" Combine this phenomenon with a more mobile and less loyal workforce, and the result for the organization can be mass exodus. Members of an academic institution that we know well left shortly after a new dean was appointed. What had once been a highly sociable, collaborative environment had changed drastically. Faculty disengaged. Arguments about priorities among senior administrators echoed in the hallways. People who once generously praised their colleagues were warned to look out for themselves. The institution had traditionally been a career-long destination, but a significant proportion of faculty exited. Some went across town to the chief competitor. One professor who stayed behind lamented, "The joy and collaborative spirit are gone. It's not a pleasant environment anymore."

Many employees who do leave eventually don't do so right away—a detail with enormous consequences. The connection between cause and effect disappears when time lags between an incident of incivility and an employee's departure. A financial manager told us he knew he had had enough after a particularly insulting comment his boss made. But he also knew that he wanted to find a really good job. Explaining his exit strategy, he noted that he "avoided [my] boss as much as I could. I did okay work, focused on my future." He persevered for another few months while he looked for a great opportunity. When we asked why he had waited so long before he left, he told us, "Why not? I had done nothing wrong. Nobody had any reason to be watching me." Even if the incivility has been reported or witnessed, if the target waits a few months before leaving (while figuring out what to do next or lining up a new job), it's unlikely that the human resources department, management, and even close colleagues will make the connection. From the organizational record and the manager's perspective, the link between incivilities and exit vanishes.

J.P., a promising employee at a hedge fund, was an honor student and class officer from a top undergraduate business school. In his short tenure with his firm, he realized that some of the investment bank's systems for booking trades were inefficient and error prone. On his own initiative, J.P. redesigned systems that led to much greater efficiencies across the firm. These changes attracted notice, and J.P. was quickly moved from the back area to the middle area (and one step closer to the trading floor!). He hit a wall with Talia, his new manager, who was known for her incivilities. Talia spewed stinging e-mails, belittling comments, and passive-aggressive power plays. She would even blow by J.P. in the hall without so much as acknowledging his greeting.

It didn't take long for J.P. to recognize that he was spending a disproportionate amount of his time trying to deal with Talia's incivilities, time he should have spent doing his job. He decided to discuss the situation with Talia's boss and eventually with the CFO. The boss seemed to shrug off J.P.'s perspective; the CFO explained that he "had bigger fish to fry," but he also promised to look out for J.P. A year later, after a lot more head banging, J.P. decided that it simply wasn't worth staying. "I don't think I can win with Talia, and nobody seems to care. Talia killed any possibility of my pursuing plum opportunities in the firm, so I'm leaving. There is an absolute correlation between uncivil dealings with my immediate manager and the decision not to make a career in this firm."

Taking a step back, J.P. articulated what we heard so many times before. Workplace incivilities push employees over the edge. J.P. confessed that he was no longer a team player, that he was playing for himself. "It's tough to measure, but it matters. Now my focus is all about leveraging myself into a better place where I don't have to deal with this." J.P. has registered to start a top M.B.A. program. When he gives notice, everyone will believe that his desire to pursue an advanced degree is the reason he is leaving. Until classes begin, he's going to put in a few more months with the investment bank, keep doing what he needs to do and collecting the pay and benefits along the way, but he's already checked out. On the basis of the loss of J.P.'s full efforts, his pending departure, plus the wake of employees who have left because of Talia's incivility, we estimate that Talia's uncivil behavior has cost the hedge fund nearly a million dollars.[8]

Rude Awakenings

- More than half the employees who are treated uncivilly consider leaving; one in eight actually does so.
- Costs of replacing employees range up to four times their annual salaries.
- When targets leave, their knowledge, "connections," and experience go out the door with them.
- When incivility drives employees away, they almost never report it as the reason for departure.
- Targets who exit often wait months before leaving. This time lag erases the links between incivility as cause and departure as effect.

10

Misery Loves Company:
The Cost to Your Reputation

Do not believe that you can possibly escape the reward of your action.

—Ralph Waldo Emerson

WHEN IT COMES to incivility, misery loves company. Disrespect among employees touches more outsiders than you might think, and its effects are greatly underestimated by organizations.

Let's begin by considering the role played by a company's reputation. A study by professors at New York University's Stern School of Business found that companies with good reputations, controlling for many other factors, had much greater profitability than the industry average, as well as greater stock values.[1] Research across business disciplines reveals that reputation affects a company's ability to recruit and retain top talent, increases sales, allows firms to charge greater prices, and attracts investors and strategic partners. Given customers' new power to shape a firm's image via blogs and other Web sites, a company's reputation seems to be more valuable, and vulnerable, than ever. In one recent study, 82 percent of financial advisers and 71 percent of high net worth investors reported believing that a significant portion of the market value of a company is based on reputation.[2]

Over the years we have found that nearly 80 percent of a company's ambassadors—i.e., employees—who are treated poorly tell people inside and outside the organization. They tell colleagues at work, and they tell their family and friends. Male targets are more likely to tell people at work—especially those below them in the hierarchy. If an offender is of lesser status, the male target will "mark" her and use her as a symbol of what lies ahead for others who might lash out at him; if an offender is of greater status, the male target will quickly spread the word about what a jerk the offender is, swaying others from working with her. Female targets of incivility are more likely to turn outside the organization, confiding in family and friends. Female targets tend to seek support from others, regain their balance, and recoup their strength so that they are ready to take recourse when the best opportunity arises.

What happens when people spread the word? Consider a situation that has developed on our own campus. One alumna we know makes a point of steering friends and fellow alums away from her own "big four" accounting/consulting firm toward one of its competitors. At an alumni dinner recently, Lauren explained that she had made a mistake choosing the firm she did. Though she acknowledged that her manager was largely to blame for how she felt, Lauren said his incivility had created a miserable culture. She was trying to save others from similar experiences, and she prayed that she could transfer to a rival firm at the end of the year. Rest assured, it doesn't take long for those messages to sweep through graduating classes.

Technology gives disgruntled employees more power than ever. Employees sometimes vent their anger by posting accounts of their experiences on the Web and by sharing evidence of the uncivil communication that set them off. In an infamous example, Neal Patterson, CEO of Cerner Corporation (a $1.5 billion company that sells software to the medical industry), arrived at work one day and found the parking lot rather empty. He had grown increasingly agitated about what he perceived to be a lack of effort, so he sent the following e-mail message to more than four hundred employees:

"We are getting less than 40 hours of work from a large number of our K.C.-based EMPLOYEES. The parking lot is sparsely used at 8 a.m.; likewise at 5 p.m. As managers—you either do not know what your EMPLOYEES are doing; or you do not CARE. You have created expectations on the work effort which allowed this to happen inside Cerner, creating a very unhealthy environment. In either case, you have a problem and you will fix it or I will replace you.

"NEVER in my career have I allowed a team which worked for me to think they had a 40-hour job. I have allowed YOU to create a culture which is permitting this. NO LONGER."

"Hell will freeze over," he vowed, before he would dole out more employee benefits. The parking lot would be his yardstick of success, he said; it should be "substantially full" at 7:30 a.m. and 6:30 p.m. on weekdays and half full on Saturdays.

"You have two weeks," he said. "Tick, tock."

Before his two-week ultimatum had even neared, the message had been posted to a Yahoo discussion group. Within three days Cerner's stock tumbled 22 percent. Patterson's personal wealth plummeted $28 million. The *Wall Street Journal*, *Financial Times*, *New York Times*, *Forbes*, and *Fortune* all ran stories on the incident. Once named by *Fortune* magazine's as one of the hundred best companies to work for, Cerner and its CEO suddenly looked terrible. Within the week, according to the *New York Times*, Patterson sent a confidential apology and confirmation of the company's work ethic problem to those he had offended.

Incivility tarnishes a firm's reputation when workers who have been mistreated take it out on customers, even if they don't mean to. Employees who attempt to shake off their uncivil experiences often carry an edge of anger, fear, or sadness. Sarah, a retail stock associate from Florida with a top-selling children's clothing store, related how her stock manager talked about employees behind their backs, made snide remarks, and blamed staff for his own shortcomings. On days when Sarah didn't encounter his rudeness, she was more productive, felt much more positive working with customers, and even helped them search for merchandise much more cheerfully. She felt a difference, and she was sure that this transferred to customers. "The whole experience was horrible, and I told myself I'd never work in retail again because of it."

Some employees admit to *intentionally* taking out their frustrations or anger on customers. More than 15 percent of targets reported that they purposely decreased customer assistance after experiencing incivility from a coworker. Some blamed the organization and wanted to exact revenge. "Hey, I was wronged," a department store retailer remarked, "so who do you think I'm going to take it out on? My boss? No. I'll give it to the next customer I think deserves it. In the meantime I won't go out of my way to serve customers."

Customers feel this lack of respect. In recent studies we conducted with Deborah MacInnis and Valerie Folkes (of the University of Southern California), more than 25 percent of customers said that it was not unusual for an employee to act rudely to them.[3] Nearly one-third said they experienced incivility at least once or twice a month. More than 25 percent thought that rude behavior from employees to customers was more common than as recently as five years ago. These experiences are prevalent in nearly every industry, with restaurants, retail, and government topping the list. Think of the Soup Nazi on *Seinfeld* or restaurants like Ed Debevic's in Chicago, a diner whose waitstaff is intentionally rude and mocks the customers. Unlike these customers, though, the customers we and others have surveyed are not amused by uncivil behavior. In a public opinion poll, almost half say they've walked out of a business because of bad service in the past year.[4]

Though rude employee behavior and its impact on customer satisfaction may not come as a surprise, our results illustrate an additional negative impact. Two-thirds of the customers we surveyed said that when they were treated uncivilly, their attitude toward the entire organization declined. More than 60 percent told us that they were less willing to use the company's products and services. More than 90 percent told others about the rudeness. When you consider that on average, customers who experience bad service tell nine or ten people, you realize that disrespectful behavior's reputational costs are no small thing.[5]

"That was when the stock market
heard you were retiring, sir."

As with employees, treating customers uncivilly can leave an organization facing public relations nightmares. "Slip up," a *BusinessWeek* reporter recently warned, "and your service snafu becomes a tale consumers tell with relish over and over again."[6] The article detailed steps consumers take to capture organizational attention from executives, like contacting CEOs directly through personal e-mail addresses. Mona Shaw, a seventy-five-year-old retired nurse and officer of her local AARP, has become a civility-seeking pop hero. Peeved by being ignored and treated rudely by employees of Comcast, the country's largest provider of cable, entertainment, and communications products and services, Mrs. Shaw returned to her local Comcast office with a hammer and whacked away at keyboards, asking, "*Now* do I have your attention?" As Mrs. Shaw was being arrested, she suffered heart problems and was taken from the scene in an ambulance. The story was picked up by the *Washington Post* and circulated over the Internet, where it garnered the attention of local, state, and national press.[7] Shaw appeared on *Good Morning America* and *Dr. Phil*, where her perspective was aired sympathetically and nationwide.

Witnessing Incivility

When we embarked on our research, we anticipated that customers who were personally treated rudely would respond strongly, spewing negativity about the offensive employee, the organization, and the brand. What surprised us was the strength of customers' reactions to the incivilities that they *witnessed*—whether between employees or between employees and other customers.

Let's take incivility witnessed between employees and other customers. We found that:

- Eighty-three percent of people surveyed described the uncivil treatment to a friend or family member.
- Fifty-five percent took on a less favorable attitude toward the company.
- Fifty percent were less willing to use the company's products and services.

Witnesses describe their attitudes with comments like "That behavior turned me completely off to ever frequenting the establishment again"; "I said to myself that this place isn't worth coming to again"; "I'm never going back, and I'm going to tell my friends to do the same"; and "I wouldn't go near that place again, even if they paid me!" In one case we know of, a teenager was attempting to buy a sweater in an expensive department store as a present for his father. He asked a store employee for help and advice. Thinking that the teenager couldn't possibly afford the sweater, the store employee took a haughty attitude and did everything possible to get the teenager out of the store. The teenager scolded the employee and reported him to a manager, who in turn forced the employee to apologize and give the teenager a discount. But this response didn't appease the customer who witnessed and told us about the incident. She "wanted to punch that employee in his face because of his rudeness," and she vowed never to return to the store.

Employee-to-employee incivility takes its toll too. A respondent described how he watched the owner of a bike shop mock the service tech with words like "How can you not know how to do this correctly?" conveyed in a sarcastic tone. The owner then rudely shoved the service tech to the side so that he could tackle the job himself. The customer was embarrassed and empathized with the service tech. He vowed never to go back to the store, not wanting to support an owner like that.

Do these little incidents really matter to the bottom line? You bet they do. To learn more about how people respond to witnessing employee-to-employee incivility, we designed an experiment in which participants were told that a marketing professor was helping a bank with an alumni credit card program.[8] Two confederates who were part of the research team presented themselves as representatives of the bank, explaining that they were gathering opinions about possible new logos and alternative finance options. During the experiment, half the participants witnessed incivility between the two bank representatives (one reprimanded the other for not presenting credit card mock-ups in the right sequence). The other group of participants witnessed no incivility. Our experimental question was whether witnessing employee-to-employee incivility would affect consumers' attitudes toward these employees, other employees of the organization, the organization itself, or the brand. The results were stunning:

- Nearly 80 percent of customers who had witnessed no employee-to-employee incivility said that they would use the firm's products and services in the future, while only 20 percent of the participants who witnessed incivility agreed to do so.
- Nearly two-thirds of the participants who had witnessed the incivility said that they would feel anxious dealing with *any* employee of this company. This large proportion of respondents regarded the entire firm as uncivil, even though they had encountered only two employees.

- Even though customers were not targets but simply witnesses to incivility, nine out of ten said that their attitude toward the uncivil employee became less favorable. Nearly half were less willing to use the company's products and services. One customer summarized: "Did she [the rude employee] think I wouldn't notice? Think again."

To get a sense of just how damaging it can be when people learn about uncivil leaders or employees, take the recent uncivil behavior of Sallie Mae's CEO and the ripple effects it had on the firm, its reputation, and its stock value. During a conference call, Sallie Mae CEO Albert Lord brusquely told one analyst that he would not entertain any more multipart questions. At the end of the call, Lord was heard using an expletive to tell another executive that he should leave. Disaster ensued. Shares plunged 20.7 percent, the worst one-day drop in the company's history. Two shareholders told the *New York Times* that the call, which was intended to win over investors, inspired a "crisis of confidence" in Lord's leadership. An Associated Press report led with "Sallie Mae's CEO probably missed the memo on proper executive etiquette, because brushing off questions and cursing in front of the company's analysts isn't the way to win over Wall Street."[9] The *New York Times* coverage was titled "After Chief Holds a Chat, Sallie Mae Stock Plunges."[10]

Why do customers react so unfavorably to incivility? One possibility is that witnessing rudeness draws enjoyment out of the customer experience and is thus upsetting. Another is that an uncivil interaction violates norms for appropriate employee behavior in a service setting; if negative exchanges are made between employees, they should be made offstage, away from customers' viewing. A third possibility reflects psychological theories of injustice. People tend to believe that all individuals deserve respect from others, so an uncivil act may trigger moral justice.

When we tested each of these three possible explanations, we found that some people claim that incivility does ruin their experience and does run counter to their expectations for good service. Yet it turned out that customers' negative responses are driven mostly by the belief that everyone deserves respect. Seeing anyone, even a stranger, treated rudely seems wrong and is upsetting. We thought there might be some instances in which customers might say, "Let her have it," or, "He had it coming." But we have yet to find them.

Many customers who witness employee-to-employee incivility leave immediately, before they even have time to buy anything. Often they vow never to return. Any astute service provider knows that losing existing customers is expensive and highly undesirable. Bain & Company research shows that when firms retain just 5 percent more of their best customers, corporate profits can be boosted 25 to 85 percent, depending on the industry. If your company is tolerating employee-to-employee incivility, our data show that customers are walking away before they even purchase something.

We hope that this review of incivility's reputational costs motivates managers and organizational leaders to minimize costs, retain positive reputation, and avoid public relations disasters by managing incivility. In case it doesn't, we'd like to take our argument one step farther and consider the upside of civility. In our studies, more than eight out of ten customers tell us that their attitude toward the company becomes more favorable when employees treat one another well. Eighty-five percent say they're *more* willing to use the company's products and services in the future. Fifty-five percent are more interested in learning about new products and services offered by the company where employees are treated well. It's tough to put a price on these benefits, but huge gains and reputational benefits are likely when customers share positive stories with others.

Witnessing employee-to-employee civility, a Starbucks customer reported, "This is how service should be at any place! It's difficult to see this behavior nowadays in the States. These employees are happy about their job and trained to behave nicely by the company. I heard that this company emphasizes the employees' behavior a lot. I think it is really a good idea." Another customer explained how refreshing it is to see employees looking out for one another. He claimed that he usually sees employees fighting or being lazy. To him, it was great to see that there are "considerate individuals who take the needs of another employee before their own." A customer who witnessed a similar interaction in a bank explained, "These people are nice, and I want to come back to this bank because they are not all robots." Another proclaimed, "Wow, this is very enjoyable . . . I can't wait to come back!"

It pays if your employees treat one another with respect. Customers who notice employees behaving kindly have even remarked to us that they wanted to work with them. "I thought that the store might be a nice place to work and that the employees seemed happy." Most of them told family members and friends about their positive feelings too. We come full circle to reputation and the priceless effect of good behavior.

Remember that your employees are your ambassadors. Their civil or uncivil behavior reflects the values of your organization. Stakeholders judge other employees, your organization, and your brand on the basis of what they see, and they adjust their purchases and their loyalty accordingly. In a service economy, goodwill is everything. It's hard to build it, but you can lose it in an instant. On this basis alone, you can't afford to do anything other than encourage a culture of positive, respectful, civil behavior.

Rude Awakenings

- Incivility scalds customer relationships and depletes the bottom line.
- Mistreated employees spread the damage by telling colleagues, family, friends, and others.
- Customers who simply witness incivility take their business elsewhere.
- Witnessing employee-to-employee incivility is as offensive to customers as being the victim of incivility.

11

Time Wounds All Heels: Even Offenders Lose

Spite and ill-nature are among the most expensive luxuries in life.

—Dr. Samuel Johnson

Losses incurred by offenders may be the last to come to mind when incivility occurs. Yet they are significant. Offenders lose support from their employees, customers, and shareholders. Their individual and team success can plummet. Their careers may derail, their reputations may be dashed, they may lose their jobs, and they might even be sued. Most offenders seem unaware of just how damaging or costly incivility is. Many appear to get away with it, at least for a while, although it always comes back to haunt them.

If offenders themselves pay a price for their uncivil conduct, it is because targets wouldn't have it any other way. Over the years, in surveys of about a thousand people across industries, we've found that 94 percent of targets get even with their offenders. There are also reputational costs that accrue when a colleague or boss is hotheaded, short-tempered, or just plain obnoxious. Consider what happened to Linda Wachner, CEO of apparel maker Warnaco. In 1992, *Fortune* magazine heralded Wachner as America's "most successful businesswoman."[1]

Unfortunately, Wachner was quietly developing a reputation for being uncivil and sometimes downright abusive. As reported in the *New York Times*, she became known for "demoralizing employees by publicly dressing them down for missing sales and profit goals or for simply displeasing her."[2] Wachner would also call an employee who had failed to please her late at night and demand that he or she meet her at the office early the next morning. When the employee showed up, Wachner would let the person sit there for long stretches of time, waiting and worrying, before dressing him or her down. Sometimes the waiting went on for the entire day. As a former executive related, "The only people who survive at Warnaco are people who were abused children."

According to insiders, Wachner's uncivil attacks and personal criticisms upset so many people that the firm experienced excessive turnover and the loss of many talented employees. Wachner's style churned the company through three chief financial officers at the Authentic Fitness division in five years, five presidents of Calvin Klein Kids in three years, and three directors of Warnaco Intimate Apparel in four years. Eventually Warnaco went bankrupt and Wachner was fired. Investors, former employees, and retail partners attribute the downfall to her unpleasant management style. As a former employee who was asked repeatedly to return to the company explained, "Linda is her own worst enemy. . . . No one who can get work elsewhere wants to put up with her."

We've discovered similar examples in our own research. Corinne, an ambitious executive administrator at a top hospital, had a habit of insulting employees during meetings and in front of their subordinates and making belittling remarks about the performances and dress of her underlings. We were told that subordinates struggled to maintain their dignity. Corinne's job eventually unraveled because she was uncivil to the top team during board meetings, working on her laptop during presentations, firing off e-mails, and focusing on her own projects instead of participating or listening to the chair and other speakers. The hospital would have been wise to pay attention to warning signs. Employees at all levels had had similar experiences with Corinne, but it wasn't until she disrespected the board that she lost her job. Corinne was stunned. She had disrespected up, down, and across, and it caught up with her. When she left, people openly celebrated.

Why do rising stars like Corinne transgress so often? As we've seen firsthand, some blindly believe that their arrogance and lack of respect for others have contributed to their success. Yet smart people who climb the ladder without respect for others learn at some point that they have succeeded *despite* their incivility, not *because* of it. A good example is the New York Giants coach Tom Coughlin. Although his team had improved under his leadership (2004–2007), his harsh style led to plenty of finger pointing and complaining. By 2007 the team was splintering, and players' confidence diminishing. Coughlin finally realized that he needed to change. He recruited a group of veteran players into a leadership group whose job it would be to disseminate his message to the rest of the team but in a more civil style. The team rallied behind the new approach. As Coughlin remarked, "The real distinguishing factor was that we just kept getting better and our confidence grew. Our players actually felt that they could win under any circumstance. Each game that we approached, they believed. We used the phrase. 'Believe it. Feel it.' And they did. We practiced that way. We prepared that way."[3] The results were stunning. Coughlin led the Giants to an improbable run to the Super Bowl and victory over the undefeated, two-time defending champion New England Patriots.

Insights into incivility's impact may be the single most important lesson we can share with fast-trackers. If you treat people badly, all the technical skills and confidence you can harness will not get you to the top. Career derailment happens all the time as ascendant managers fail to live up to their full potential. Numerous studies have shown that the number one characteristic associated with an executive's failure is "an insensitive, abrasive or bullying style," while the second is "aloofness or arrogance."[4] It's easy to see why. While cunning power plays can force compliance, insensitivity often fosters a lack of support in crucial situations. Subordinates fail to relay important information, sabotage efforts or resources, and stop generating top-notch ideas.[5] Sooner or later rude people sabotage their own success.

Even if incivility doesn't lead directly to the offender's derailment, it certainly doesn't help his or her career. People eagerly wait for offenders to fail and may look for opportunities to help push them over the edge. All our survey studies and experiments lead to the same conclusion: Targets refuse to help offenders. They also neither trust nor like people who tolerate incivility in others under their control. One-third of targets refuse to work with their offenders; many others just stop performing for them. Seventeen percent intentionally deny or remove a benefit from offenders, and more than one-third purposely fail to transmit information. While it is difficult to attach a dollar figure to some of these losses, there's no question that these actions limit offenders' potential efficiency and effectiveness.

As the adage goes, "Friends come and friends go, but enemies accumulate." The experience of a senior VP at a Fortune 50 company brings this truth to life. Although he was by far the best vice president this organization had ever had, he was also a little Napoleon, abrasive in meetings and dismissive of junior employees. After working with his team to develop ideas, this offender would never speak up or take responsibility if the CEO tore into their presentation; he let the team fry alone. Not surprisingly, when the offender himself was caught for having committed a company no-no, all support vanished immediately, especially in his division. "It wasn't that he wasn't a smart guy," one of the firm's senior HR executives told us. "They absolutely loved his strategy. But his uncivil behavior caught up with him. His own people weren't willing to support him, and ultimately he was fired."

Another example this HR executive shared involved Jake, a top executive and heir apparent to the chief operating officer position. Jake was known for his propensity to tear people apart. Nonetheless, Marcus, the current COO, recognized Jake's talent and thought he could handle the COO's job. He offered to coach Jake on his people skills. At a dinner meeting, the COO asked Jake, "How many times have you asked a question at a meeting that you didn't know the answer to?" Jake smirked, shrugging. The COO pressed: "When was the last time?" Jake just started to laugh. There was not *one* time. His arrogance shone through again. Eventually everyone, including the COO, ruled Jake out as the successor. His uncivil style had derailed his career.

Even if a rude person manages to climb the ladder in his organization, his reputation may quash opportunities elsewhere. *USA Today* featured a story about the Waiter Rule, one of those must-dos that every CEO learns on the way up.[6] The idea is this: How people treat big shots matters relatively little, but how they treat the waiter "is like a magical window into the soul." Raytheon CEO Bill Swanson documents this in *Swanson's Unwritten Rules of Management*. "Watch out for people," he writes, "who have a situational value system, who can turn the charm on and off depending on the status of the person they are interacting with. Be especially wary of those who are rude to people perceived to be in subordinate roles." Au Bon Pain cofounder Ron Shaich, now CEO of Panera Bread, related his experience with this while interviewing a candidate for general counsel. The candidate was charming to Shaich but rude to someone cleaning the tables. She didn't get the job.[7]

Legendary basketball coach John Wooden described an interview with a talented player to whom he was prepared to offer a scholarship. During a visit to the player's home, the young man's mother politely asked Wooden a question. Her son looked at her and snapped, "How can you be so ignorant? Just keep your mouth shut and listen to what Coach says." Wooden found the player's behavior completely unacceptable. "If he couldn't respect her, how could he possibly respect me when things got tough?" Coach Wooden ended the meeting politely and did not offer the scholarship. This player went on to be an extremely successful player with a top program. He even helped his team beat UCLA on more than one occasion. Nonetheless, as Coach Wooden said, "[I was] delighted that I had discovered something so important before it was too late, before allowing him to contaminate our team with his 'values.'"[8]

Managers have also told us that they heard about an offender's reputation for incivility just before the final decision and then retracted the offer. Often people come forward after an uncivil individual becomes a finalist. Even after a lengthy search, as word of the candidacy gets out and the reality of the future with this person comes into focus, bad news catches up with the offender. A talented radiologist had an attractive offer in hand and was ready to join a prestigious hospital. His record and background were impressive; he had passed through the interviews with other doctors without any issues. Yet after learning of the offer, an administrative assistant remarked that she thought there were some issues with the candidate: Frankly, he seemed uncivil. Her boss asked her to follow her hunch. Through a trail of personal contacts, she learned that the doctor had left a wake of targets in his previous position. The hiring executive acted swiftly. He told the candidate that it was not in his interest to accept, as the incivility that had surfaced would sour the deal and mark the candidate's record.

People get even with offenders in ways that are more or less direct, intentionally or not. An attorney told us how lawyers who are uncivil to staff often destroy their own cases. As he put it, "A lawyer relies on his staff. People won't work as hard or prepare as well if they're upset with him." A paralegal told us about a partner with a top firm in the Southeast who was uncivil. He burned through paralegals, assistants, and associates, and it became a running joke. What wasn't funny was the negative effect this had on work produced by others. People didn't work as hard for the offender; they didn't run with as many leads, push to gather extra evidence, or check details as diligently. In addition, attorneys attended fewer networking functions (where new business was thought to be drummed up) for the sole reason that they didn't want to be near the partner.

Justice Gary Hastings (of the Los Angeles County Superior Court and the California Court of Appeal) shared with us an interesting story about the effects of lawyers' incivility on jurors in a case he had presided over. Hank Gathers was a personable all-American basketball player at Loyola Marymount University in Los Angeles. During the 1988–1989 season, he became the second player in history to lead NCAA Division I in scoring and rebounding in the same season. He was diagnosed with an abnormal heartbeat and prescribed a beta-blocker after collapsing in a game on December 9, 1989. However, LMU coaches thought that the medication adversely affected his play, and they cut back his dosage. On March 4, 1990, Gathers collapsed again during a West Coast Conference tournament game and died, despite frantic attempts made to revive him. His family filed a $32.5 million negligence suit against his coach, the university, and a dozen other university officials and doctors, charging them with responsibility for Gathers's death from heart failure. LMU settled out of court for an undisclosed amount.

Justice Hastings detailed the backgrounds of three attorneys who tried the case. Bruce Fagel, representing the Gathers family, was a medical doctor as well as a prestigious lawyer with an impressive record. Marshall Silverberg, representing one of the attending physicians, had both an impressive court record and a photographic memory. Finally, according to Hastings, attorney Craig Dummit, who represented a doctor at LMU, wasn't really famous for much of anything.

During the lengthy juror selection process, each potential juror completed an eight- to ten-page questionnaire. In making selections, attorney Fagel grew frustrated. When asked whether he'd like to select someone else to be questioned for possible inclusion in the jury, he snapped, "No. I don't want to give Mr. Silverberg time to memorize the person's survey." Silverberg immediately volleyed, "I already have," and picked up questioning in excruciating detail without a moment's hesitation. Throughout the proceedings, Fagel and Silverberg displayed remarkable knowledge and talent, peppered with rude cracks and curt responses. Dummit didn't do much of anything notable.

Ultimately the case was dismissed. But what shocked Hastings was what he learned after the trial, when he listened to the jurors: "You know who they said the best attorney in the courtroom was? Dummit. Every juror agreed." Hastings asked why. Jurors told him that Dummit wasn't flashy and that he didn't show up the witnesses or the opposing attorneys. He was civil, respecting everyone. The members of the jury confided that the other two attorneys—the gifted, high-powered ones— had lost the jurors' favor because of their incivilities.

According to Carla Christofferson, a partner with the L.A. firm O'Melveny & Myers (and co-owner of the WNBA's Los Angeles Sparks), a reputation for civility and character are everything. Even in a city as big as Los Angeles, attorneys argue before the same judges, compete against the same attorneys (who at some level they also have to work with), and gain or lose business on the basis of their reputations and the outcomes associated with behaving respectfully. Christofferson shared a story about how her civil behavior had affected a jury. Christofferson had injured her foot and after a lapse in a trial had returned without her boot cast. When members of the jury saw her in the hall, they approached her and said, "Awww . . . that's great. You got your cast off!" She knew that the jury didn't have that affection for the opposing side; its attorneys had been bickering with one another. So she wasn't surprised later that day when the jury returned with a high award for her side and against the other, uncivil side.

Civility matters to defendants too. A study conducted at a court in Red Hook, New York, found that a lawyer who is civil and explains things clearly is much more likely to have a happier defendant, *regardless of the outcome of the case.* Commenting on this outcome, Judge Hastings noted: "The atmosphere of the court room is very important. If the judge or lawyers are surly, then jurors get a bad vibe and both parties end up unhappy. . . . If the judge is a jerk on the bench, then both parties may feel like they're not getting a fair trial. . . . If you don't have civility, you can be doing everything appropriately, but people won't believe they got a fair shake and they'll be very upset. This dramatically increases the chances for appeal."

At the very least, incivility sparks mean-spirited gossip about the offender. In our research, nearly two-thirds of targets reported telling a neutral party about uncivil behavior so that they could get even with the offender. These stories tend to be filled with rich negative detail as targets recall each uncivil phrase and rude act. People reported saving e-mails so that they could remember dialogue and setting while regaling listeners inside and outside their organizations. And once an offender develops a reputation for rudeness or emotional volatility, it's as if that individual has been branded. Isabelle, a top executive whom we've worked with, had a really difficult time because of this. Despite her hard work with personal coaches and the progress she had made toward positive changes, people still saw her as uncivil. Employees couldn't seem to let go of their memories of her mistreatment and were slow to forgive. This paralyzed Isabelle in her organization. Even when her reports produced results for her, they did so begrudgingly, turning their shoulder on her pet projects and failing to deliver as much as they could have.

Medicine offers fascinating examples about how offenders pay for incivility. As one research study shows,[9] people tend to file malpractice suits because of poor medical care *and* how the patient feels about the doctor. Alice Burkin, a medical malpractice lawyer, described a case in which the patient wanted to sue her internist for the delayed diagnosis of a breast tumor when the radiologist was the one at fault. Why? Because the internist was rude. As Burkin reflected, "[T]he doctors who don't [treat people civilly] are the ones who get sued."[10] A patient whose surgery was botched confirmed this, telling us that she "appreciated the way the doctor treated me with respect. He admitted the mistake, took responsibility, and explained several options." Because of the respect shown in this process, the patient (an attorney) decided not to sue. The managing director of a health care consulting firm we know insists that coaching doctors to be respectful and accept accountability helps avoid malpractice suits. Otherwise, she said, "The patient and his or her family will definitely make them pay."

The research study cited above compared the conversations of doctors who get sued often with those of doctors who have never been sued.[11] Those who had never been sued talked to their patients longer (an average of three minutes), but there was no difference in the amount or quality of information given or in the details given about medication or in the patient's condition. It was *how* the doctors talked to their patients that mattered.

As medical malpractice attorney Jeffrey Allen related, one of the things he and his colleagues try to find out in a deposition is what effect the doctor is likely to have on the jury. That helps them decide whether to settle or try a case. "If the doctor is arrogant, the jury will hate him. That affects not only the amount we'll seek in a settlement, but also how we'll try the case if it doesn't settle. In some cases, the doctor is such a piece of work that we'll call him as a witness even before we put our client on the stand. We hope he'll make the jury so angry that our case becomes relatively easy."

Digging deeper, psychologist Nalini Ambady and her colleagues captured thin slices of conversations between surgeons and patients. They then had judges watch the tapes and rate the doctors on the basis of warmth, hostility, dominance, and anxiousness. On the basis of those ratings alone, Ambady could predict which surgeons got sued and which didn't.[12] Malcolm Gladwell summarizes this phenomenon eloquently in his book *Blink*: "Malpractice sounds like one of those infinitely complicated and multidimensional problems. But in the end it comes down to a matter of respect, and the simplest way that respect is communicated is through tone of voice, and the most corrosive tone of voice that a doctor can assume is a dominant tone."[13]

Research in other fields confirms this. In education, four-minute clips showing college teachers in action could be used to predict the teachers' rankings on evaluations for a full-semester course.[14] Even research using short, silent video clips revealed that people's ratings of the teachers on characteristics like dominance, warmth, anxiousness, professionalism, and supportiveness accurately predicted student evaluations.[15] Such ratings did not reflect the teacher's physical attractiveness, as has sometimes been assumed. Rather, they seemed to draw on behavioral information. Historical lessons described in the Appendix apply here as well: Voice tone, intonation, and body language carry social implications. We'd add serious business consequences.

As we've seen in this chapter, uncivil offenders may think they're getting away with the rudeness they spew toward others, but in fact it costs them greatly. An array of empirical and anecdotal evidence shows that targets don't forget. Payback may come immediately or when offenders least expect it, and it may be intentional or unconscious. Incivility colors people's perceptions of the offender in deep and meaningful ways. Once colored, these perceptions are difficult to erase. Research and numerous examples across industries tell us so. So to all those offenders out there, we ask you: Is it really worth it?

Rude Awakenings

- Ninety-four percent of targets take action to get even with their offenders.
- Eighty-six percent of targets go out of their way to avoid their offenders. About a third refuse to work with the offender; many others just stop performing for her.
- Uncivil people put their professional reputations at risk. Nine out of ten targets tell someone about the offender's incivility; two out of three will tell a neutral party in an effort to damage the offender's reputation.
- People skills become more important the higher up you go. They can stop your ascent or keep you climbing.

PART III

The Solution

12

Success! How Five Organizations Have Set the Course

The purest treasure mortal times afford
Is spotless reputation. . . .

—William Shakespeare

IN THIS CHAPTER, we consider best practices by offering glimpses inside five very different organizations, Cisco, Starbucks, the health care services firm DaVita, Microsoft, and O'Melveny & Myers, the successful international law firm. Although these firms vary by size, industry, locations, and business objectives, each of them is cultivating civility within its workplace, and each attributes at least some part of its success to that fact. The steps these firms have taken span the entire human resources cycle; in essence, these firms have decided that it's better (and cheaper!) to curtail or prevent incivility throughout an employee's tenure than to fix it once it takes hold.

CISCO SYSTEMS

In 2008, Cisco was recognized by *Fortune* as eighteenth among the Top 20 Most Admired Companies in the United States. In the categories of people management and quality, it came in at number one. But those were not Cisco's only accolades from *Fortune*. It was also ranked sixth among the 2008 list of 100 Best Companies to Work For. Cisco has a voluntary turnover rate of only 4 percent. Nearly half a million people vie annually for an opportunity to become a member of the Cisco Systems organization.

The company attributes its success to a positive work environment that enables employees to perform at their best. To the best of our knowledge, Cisco is the first corporation ever to institute a formal program focused on civility. The stated goal of its global civility program is "to help Employees recognize and report incidents that may cause disruption or threaten safety, and Managers to identify, address and resolve circumstances that fall within the broad spectrum of Workplace Civility." The program utilizes specific levers to foster civility and curtail the occurrence or escalation of rudeness.

First, detailed guidelines help managers and human resources experts recognize and respond to signs of escalating incivility. Managers are instructed on how to ask appropriately probing questions (e.g., "What did you mean when you said . . . ?") when confronted with direct or veiled threats, blaming, anger, or intimidation. To reinforce civility and reduce any escalating incivility, Cisco trains managers and human resources experts through case studies, experiential activities, group discussions, coaching, and video presentations. There's also a self-study playbook or road map that provides detailed information on civility, incivility, and the escalation of incivility, as well as processes for resolution. A Web-based resource center provides detailed processes, worksheets, preparatory guides, and checklists of references (e.g., legal services and employee assistance programs). Finally, Cisco has developed a team approach to reduce overreactions, underreactions, and unnecessary workplace disruptions. As part of this approach, experts come together to assess the situation whenever incivility escalates.

The civility program aligns with a strong culture of mutual respect. Cisco built that culture by consistently recruiting the right employees, setting clear expectations, training employees in civility, and role modeling appropriate, civil behavior. Cisco's management believes that violations of its code of conduct, with or without apparent malicious intent, can interfere with its productive work environment. When any transgressions occur, the civility program gives managers what they need to assess the situation, confer with experts, and provide timely decisions and guidance to contain and curtail incivility.

At Cisco, an unflinching focus on civility pays off.

STARBUCKS

Over the years clients have told us that they believe their companies are changing so fast that it's impossible to keep their values on track. Few have experienced the kind of change that Starbucks has. In 2006, Starbucks added an average of five new stores and two hundred employees per day, seven days per week, as it expanded in thirty-six countries. Understandably, one of Starbucks' thorniest challenges is maintaining a consistent level of product and service delivery. As David Pace, vice president of partner resources, explained, "The challenge for us is to build and sustain the culture . . . we have to take a somewhat similar approach [across all stores] where we tell the people that are here what we expect. We try to help them understand and relate to the kind of culture that we're trying to create."[1]

Civility comes in everywhere. Starbucks spreads the word about desired values with its mission statement, six guiding principles. The first principle speaks to the essence of achieving civility: "Provide a great work environment and treat each other with respect and dignity." But words are never enough. As Pace explains, "I don't think you can just come along for a ride on this one at the senior level. You have to believe it. Your CEO and chairman and other senior leaders within the organization have to live it." Starbucks's clear mission evolved very early because founder Howard Schultz understood the worth of written values. Today even Schultz acknowledges that the words may not be unique, but he and his top executives see as different the level of attention that Starbucks gives to those values. "We use it as a living document," Pace adds. "It is clearly . . . our Constitution, our Bill of Rights."

Like any values statement, the guiding principles would be useless if employees throughout the company did not understand and adhere to them. So every day, as many new "partners" (Starbucks's term for employees at all levels, anywhere in the organization) join its organization, the company makes sure that each of them is briefed on the principles and how they are put into action. Since store managers serve as the primary role models in the stores, they receive behavioral skills training on how to deliver partner-centric, customer-centric behavior. In addition to day-to-day conduct, Starbucks reinforces partner-centric values through affordable health care, stock options, and tuition reimbursement. What makes these perks unusual at Starbucks is that the leaders view them as investments rather than costs. "Many organizations talk about [investing in employees]," Pace says. "We actually, truly live that relationship."

To assure that store managers are respectful and civil, Starbucks sends them to an annual leadership conference at which the guiding principles are reviewed and discussed. The conference doesn't just focus on how to treat customers, as we find in many service organizations. It helps store managers learn and practice the best ways of treating their employees and one another. Mission Review is another tool that keeps employees' eyes on civility. Through Mission Review, the company encourages partners to submit feedback about any workplace behaviors that go against Starbucks's guiding principles. To encourage honest feedback, partners are free to share their perspectives anonymously. More than typical employee suggestion boxes, Mission Review is a conduit for ongoing 360-degree feedback to assure civility at Starbucks.

If rankings and other data are any indication, Starbucks's efforts to deliver on its core value of civility are paying off. In 2007, it placed second in *Fortune*'s list of America's Most Admired Companies and first in the food service industry. It was first among the "Most Admired" in categories of "People Management" and "Quality of Management." In 2008, *BusinessWeek* named Starbucks number sixteen among The Best 50 Performers, despite a nosedive in share value in the previous twelve months, adding that "[a] weaker Starbucks is still a pretty good business." When Starbucks slipped to number six among *Fortune*'s Most Admired Companies in 2008, even critics were quick to note that the drop was a reflection of overexpansion and in no way signaled any decline in popularity of the firm among job applicants. That perspective is borne out in Starbucks's number seven ranking among the Best Companies to Work For of 2008 and in the statistic that voluntary turnover among Starbucks's nearly two hundred thousand employees is below 15 percent. Finally, we'd note that last year the company received an incredible seven hundred thousand applicants for twenty-five hundred new jobs.

Behind the Starbucks numbers are great stories. Recently one of our respondents watched one of Starbucks's frontline employees approach a female colleague and ask about her day. The colleague told him that she was tired and sad. He comforted her and made her laugh, and she thanked him for his consideration. As our respondent noted, "They continued working, but both of them had smiles. I think this indicates how a positive, happy work environment is helpful. I should tell you that my coffee tasted even better than usual. In fact I could imagine myself working there."

What better testimony is there to the power of civility?

DAVITA INC.

DaVita dialysis services provides health care to more than one hundred thousand patients with chronic kidney failure; its facilities are located in more than seven hundred hospitals in forty-three states. DaVita has been recognized by *Fortune* as one of the Top 10 Most Admired Health Care Companies, and by AARP as a Best Employer for Workers over 50. *Training* magazine selected it as one of the Training Top 100. But it wasn't always that way. When Kent Thiry came on board as CEO in October 1999, the organization was a mess. Thiry explained that DaVita was "technically bankrupt": "It was being investigated by the SEC, sued by shareholders, had turnover at over twice the current levels, was almost out of cash, and, in general, wasn't the happiest of places."[2]

Even though DaVita (then named Total Renal Care) was in a precarious financial position, Thiry and the new management team he brought with him focused on business results and culture. At the root of improvements they knew that they had to create something, a culture or community bigger than they were. Thiry and his team set out to build a strong positive values-based organization because he believed it was a means to building a healthy community.

DaVita's leadership team believed not only that a positive, respectful community would be good for employees and business but that it was also directly tied to the goal of their business-patient well-being. The team recognized the power of emotional contagion (which we discuss in Chapter Eight) and how positive emotions and respect improve patient satisfaction, attitudes, well-being, and perhaps, survival. In 2000, Total Renal Care took its first strategic step by developing its mission and values statement. Along the way, teammates and management deliberated together to choose a new name, DaVita, an Italian term that translates roughly as "giving life."[3]

Like Starbucks, DaVita takes company values to heart. It sets an industry standard for socializing employees toward civility and mutual respect. As Bill "Coach" Shannon, senior vice president and chief wisdom officer, told us, "We view ourselves as a community first and a company second." By changing its name and referring to the organization as a village, DaVita highlights its goal of creating a tight-knit, friendly community of physicians, clinicians, and other health care teammates who work together to enhance patient care. Take a tour of the main offices, and you'll rarely hear the word "company" spoken at all. Agenda items for meetings include "state of the village," while the chairman and CEO, Kent Thiry, has an alternative job title on his office door, MAYOR, DAVITA VILLAGE. Borrowing from *The Three Musketeers*, DaVita features "One for All, and All for One" on banners in corporate headquarters and as a theme for training events at DaVita Academy.

Like Starbucks, DaVita hires with its values firmly in mind. As Shannon described it, "By the time you get to our group, I know you've been vetted in terms of qualifications. Now it's all about whether you seem to fit the DaVita values." Even for those already inside the organization, adherence to values is always under close watch. Periodic satisfaction surveys elicit general feedback: Is the company living up to its values?

How about your teammates? And your manager? Teammates with low scores must comply with a development plan, and all employees are expected to address weak areas. Employees at the manager level and above receive a mission and values report card every year that includes self-assessment as well as assessment by their direct reports. Even Thiry is evaluated by fourteen people, and the results go straight to the board of directors without any editing.[4] Those at vice president and senior vice president levels are required to complete 360-degree assessments at least every two years. Most opt to do so annually.

Live the values, and you'll be rewarded well at DaVita. Shannon told us, "We identify shining stars of the values through nominations. They're invited to meet with senior management. They're treated like VIPs, and remember, they're selected solely for modeling our values. It has nothing to do with who's the fastest or the most efficient technician." In fact DaVita does not reward employees on standard metrics of revenue or productivity; all incentives are strictly values related.

The many investments that DaVita makes in professional and personal development are based on the company's values. The firm's orientation program, DaVita Academy, draws participants from every level of the organization. As part of this two-day program, the CEO and other senior executives talk about value-related topics like teammate dynamics and conflict resolution. New employees take personality tests to learn more about themselves and how their styles affect their relationships with others. To strengthen their individual connections to the village, academy participants are encouraged to create personal credos that flow from DaVita's mission, values, and beliefs. As Shannon put it, "We want people to feel comfortable here, empowered, and believing that they can make a difference."

The socialization at the academy cuts costs. Those who attend have a much lower turnover rate within their first six months. Among the thirty-one hundred people who went through the academy socialization last year, only eleven left. Executives at DaVita report that employees who participate in academy socialization are more than fifty times more likely to stay with the company.

Focusing on values has paid off in remarkable ways for DaVita. Between 1999 and 2005 the company's market capitalization grew from less than a quarter million dollars to more than five billion. Clinical outcomes are now the best in the industry, and there's been a 50 percent reduction in turnover.[5] Stock has jumped more than tenfold since Thiry came on board and initiated this focus on values.[6]

At DaVita, it's all about company values that center on civility, and that has certainly paid off.

MICROSOFT

For eleven consecutive years, Microsoft has been on *Fortune*'s list of the top hundred companies to work for. As a long-term employee stated proudly, "If you want to impact the world with software, there is no better place to be." Microsoft boasts smart people and a rich, challenging work environment. The software king is extraordinarily generous to its employees and to society, offering an exceptional health insurance plan (zero premiums, no deductibles), extraordinary employee perks, and world-class philanthropy (highlighted, of course, through the personal generosity of the Gates family). In 2007, the Harris Interactive poll ranked Microsoft number one in corporate reputation, with additional enviable marks for leadership and financial results.

It's unusual for a highly successful company to take a critical look at itself, but that's just what Microsoft did in 2003. Leaders recognized a perception problem: Microsoft had become a company that people loved to hate. Customer data pointed toward arrogance. Microsoft was seen as uncivil. Insiders sensed a growing discrepancy between the Microsoft culture portrayed in the mission statement and the way life really was. Carrie Olesen, Microsoft's director of employee capability and empowerment, summed it up: "We had a bunch of smart people [who] didn't need civility. . . . We were busy winning." That was okay for the early years, but Microsoft's business was changing. Success no longer hinged on selling a product in a box. Instead customer contact was key. Leaders at Microsoft knew they had to change customer perceptions, and they knew that changes had to start from the inside. To address the growing discrepancy, Microsoft conducted an extensive culture assessment, complete with projections that reached out thirty years, to develop its "leadership blueprint," a document that outlined the culture it aspired to achieve. Everything was up for grabs, from the selection processes to the assessment and feedback tools to training, learning, and development—anything that affected the goal of aligning processes to achieve the desired culture.

Today top executives at Microsoft see the results of a complete cultural transformation. What's changed, precisely? Well, now Microsoft selects for corporate values rather than merely for competencies. We asked Microsoft what it looks for when hiring new employees, and its answers were full of important details. Those who make it to top candidate status behave in ways that align with Microsoft's new values. They:

- Listen to understand others' perspectives without interrupting
- Integrate diverse perspectives when making decisions
- Communicate critical feedback respectfully
- Consider the experience and knowledge of others
- Do not disparage others
- Assume the best motives in others
- Ask difficult questions to discover answers, but never to demean
- Never act in a manner that could be perceived as threatening, intolerant, or discriminatory
- Demonstrate more interest in finding the right answer than in defending a position
- Maintain objectivity when conflict arises

Recognizing that it cuts costs when employees behave respectfully is a first step. But Microsoft has gone much further to create a more civil environment. It has invested heavily in relevant selection tools and techniques that will help it choose candidates whose values match the new corporate values. Leaders at Microsoft are convinced already that there is a positive return on that investment.

Microsoft has also revamped its entire learning and development program with a focus on civility as open and respectful interactions. To get there, the firm had to streamline, adapting and dropping courses so that all training would align with the new cultural initiative. We were told that civility plays a major role in the Precision Questioning class, a popular course among new employees. Here participants learn to question their own ideas, building emotional agility and calm even in high-intensity situations. To retain civility, participants are taught in other classes how to improve their abilities to listen and appreciate healthy, constructive criticism. Overall, Microsoft's training instills the notion that civility is the currency for designing the best product possible.

Microsoft has overhauled its orientation programs as well. As in many organizations, newcomers used to spend much of their first day filling out paperwork, a practice that did nothing to reinforce their sense of connection to the firm. Now employees begin their jobs with an overview of the culture and a realistic preview of what it's like to work at Microsoft. They learn how the business is evolving and why employees are key. The new orientation approach welcomes employees as a source of change, celebrating what they bring in terms of new thinking and innovation. As part of the realistic preview, videos played during orientation tell stories about employees and the organization, from the latest innovations to how some employees actually manage a work-life balance. There are demonstrations of the newest technologies, including customer uses and future trends. New employees also learn all about Microsoft's role in giving back to communities, something that relates to corporate values. To enrich the process, employees who have worked at Microsoft for just three months visit the orientations to share their experiences and give advice to the newbies. This early-stage networking goes far in establishing a learning, friendly, civil culture. Managers are invited into the orientation process too, to remind them regularly of their instrumental roles as coaches and the company's expectation that they will act as civil, caring role models.

Employee satisfaction at Microsoft has skyrocketed since the initiative got under way. The orientation and career development programs contribute to Microsoft's extremely low attrition rate in the single digits. Managers too say that the changes have been great; the expectations they face are now much clearer. Of course it doesn't hurt that managers are getting happier, better-oriented employees to work with.

Civility is embedded in Microsoft's core competencies, and it plays a big part in feedback and rewards. Every professional competency model across the organization includes four targets: interpersonal awareness, confidence, cross-boundary collaboration, and impact and influence. All these are facilitated by civility while serving to enhance it. Those at the top of the organization are expected to display "executive maturity," including a "voice of reason," which is an awareness of their own feelings, thoughts, and hot buttons, as well as an understanding of others' behaviors. At all levels, evaluation and rewards reflect respect and civility, from "confidence" to "interpersonal awareness." Employees are rated for "challenging others respectfully when [they] disagree with them." They're evaluated on their abilities to listen, understand, and appreciate others' perspectives and behaviors.

When Microsoft provides feedback from subordinates, a great deal of attention is paid to civility. Rather than simply share verbatim open-ended comments, HR coaches work with managers to overcome their individual weaknesses. The coaches invest time and expertise to merge feedback with their own insights into high potential leaders, thus enabling leaders to accurately pinpoint efficient routes for improvement. Time, energy, and expertise guide Microsoft's employees and leaders toward being civil and managing for civility.

To gauge whether the new culture is having a positive effect, Microsoft has tracked employee satisfaction, focusing on career development. The firm sees satisfaction as a key driver of discretionary effort, creativity, and innovation and also regards it as something that enhances collaboration and dedication among employees. The data show dramatic improvement in employee and customer satisfaction, which Microsoft in turn credits for its continued revenue and market growth.

To turn around its uncivil reputation, Microsoft broadened its definition of customer satisfaction to include behavioral interaction. Now, when customers rate their experiences, they consider technical product innovation, financial value, and the engagement process. Since Microsoft initiated this facet of satisfaction into its top leaders' annual goals in 2003, effects have successfully cascaded through the organization, including measurements within annual performance reviews. Clear expectations, developmental support, and measuring and rewarding relevant results have improved customer and partner satisfaction. Focused on civility and openness, Microsoft's changes for continuous improvement have paid off.

O'MELVENY & MYERS, LLP

For more than a decade, we've studied civility and incivility through the eyes of attorneys and judges via interviews, discussion groups, and questionnaires. Additionally, we've worked with the American Bar Association and conducted state-level professional certification programs, all to enhance civility in the practice of law. Despite the vibrant sniping and one-upping in television shows like *Boston Legal*, *Law & Order*, *L.A. Law*, and *CSI*, those who practice law in the real world are at the cutting edge when it comes to understanding civility's nature, impact, and value. We close this chapter with details about O'Melveny & Myers, LLP (OMM), an organization of more than a thousand lawyers who work out of thirteen offices worldwide.

Unlike at Microsoft, the transformation at O'Melveny & Myers wasn't optional. About five years ago members of this very successful firm needed to remedy what they saw as a culture of cynicism. But before any changes were begun, perspectives were sought broadly through employee discussions. What emerged was a three-pronged approach: A more positive, civil culture would be driven by values targeting excellence, leadership, and superior citizenship. Civility entered under the prong of superior citizenship, defined specifically as "respect" and "collegiality."

After determining shared objectives, leaders at OMM pinpointed where incivility was occurring and started remedial action. Carla Christofferson, OMM partner and head of the Los Angeles office, recalls: "People were extremely leery of upward evaluations, yet it really worked."

Feedback was collected anonymously and then consolidated across respondents. To protect lower-level respondents from retribution for any criticisms, their open-ended feedback was summarized rather than shared verbatim. The result was a spectacular 97 percent response rate. On the basis of the feedback, offenders were singled out for coaching and counseling, interventions that proved highly effective. To capture the attention of the worst, most habitual offenders, warnings detailed how their shares would be reduced if their behaviors didn't improve. Most offenders' behaviors changed immediately. Only two individuals resisted, and their shares were reduced. For both, the cost incurred led quickly to significant and dramatic behavioral improvements.

Even people who already behaved well benefited from the firm's civility initiatives. Christofferson received feedback indicating that she was well liked and very respectful of others. Some of her colleagues even noted that they were impressed by her concerns about subordinates' long hours and her desire to make sure that everyone had a life outside work. But one respondent criticized her inability to apply these values in her own life. Christofferson told us, "That feedback changed my life." Her endless hours on the job had served as an example that nobody wanted to live up to. Recognizing that this pattern could lead to higher stress and greater incivility across the firm, Christofferson changed her ways, spending more time away from the office and limiting her weekend work to tasks that could be done from home.

Aside from weeding out existing incivility, OMM took steps to improve career-planning procedures and provide clearer guidelines and feedback about partnership opportunities. This included doing the right thing by providing tough but honest advice to those who were not going to make it to partner status. To ease departures, OMM created an internal Web site with job postings from client organizations. It also initiated two- and three-day retreats focused on respect and civility-related topics like "managing people." New attorneys were taught the reasons why civility matters in the practice of law. They were reminded what a small world they worked in and that they would not want to be remembered most for behaving badly.

To reinforce the new cultural values, OMM instituted awards for staff-, associate-, and partner-level employees who most adhered to the cultural values of excellence, leadership, and superior citizenship. Notable among recipients are people who teach and mentor their colleagues and commit their energies to worthy pro bono causes. OMM has also strengthened its mentoring programs by adding activities like hiking and ice cream happy hours; some of the events include employees' children. "This is so much fun," Christofferson says, "that they're having an eighth-floor reunion this year. Half the people who started this activity are still there, half aren't, but even those that aren't there are coming back for the event. Some are even flying in for it." OMM knows that these kinds of investments in community pay off. They lead to higher morale and a greater sense of collegiality for both those who have stuck with the firm and those who have left but continue to conduct their new employers' business with OMM.

After four years of edging toward greater civility, efforts are paying off. Associate-level employees at OMM are much more likely to extend their stay until their fifth or sixth year, meaning significant cost savings for the firm. When employees do leave, they are less likely to go to a competitor and more likely to join a client firm, a change that OMM encourages. Departing employees report being happier about their experiences at OMM. Enhanced civility has helped increase the percentage of female and minority associates by nearly 10 percent and boosted the representation of women and minorities at the partner level by nearly 20 percent. OMM also reports a significant decrease in its "regretted losses" (i.e., attorneys whom they wanted to keep but lost to competitors).

The firm's reputation has benefited too from its new, sharper focus on civility. OMM ranks among America's Top 20 Most Prestigious Law Firms and has received international accolades of "Best U.S. Law Firm in London" and "China Practice of the Year." Today it boasts lawyers that bring "common sense and civility . . . to important conversations." Carla Christofferson tells us that these accomplishments didn't happen overnight, but that they were worth the effort. "The biggest improvements have come in the last year," she notes, "which I think shows that it all takes time for things to take hold. I really believe there is no quick fix. You just need to keep pounding away, all the time, every year."

For O'Melveny & Myers, the relentless pursuit of civility has paid off.

———————

The success stories in this chapter come from companies that regard civility as part of their DNA. Despite diverse challenges, these firms are building and reinforcing civility as their way of doing business. Of course there's no single "right way" to get there. There's a good chance that some of the specific approaches adapted by Cisco, Starbucks, DaVita, Microsoft, and O'Melveny & Myers would be unsuitable or undesirable for your organization. The strategies, timing, and progression need to be custom tailored to your own environment, resources, and desired outcomes. Yet one feature of these stories is worth noting: The successes here have come about via a series of relatively small steps taken consistently and relentlessly. That is how any company creates and sustains a civil workplace.

13

Top Ten Things a Firm Should Do to Create a Civil Workplace

The world is a dangerous place to live; not because of the people who are evil, but because of the people who don't do anything about it.

—Albert Einstein

IT's NOT HARD to find pop advice about managing incivility. What's different here is that our recommendations are grounded in hard evidence—interviews and survey results with thousands of targets of incivility, not to mention discussions, focus groups, and interviews with hundreds of executives and managers. Though firms differ in how they structure anti-incivility policies, we have identified ten actions that *all* firms should take to encourage civil behavior and ensure a productive and positive culture, irrespective of size or industry. We've seen these guidelines work again and again. We urge you to put them into practice and take advantage of their potency.

1. SET ZERO-TOLERANCE EXPECTATIONS

When expectations flow from the top, they have the power to shape behavior and set the general tenor of a firm's culture. Executives should commit to civility standards and then articulate them frequently, both in person and in writing. Promulgating an organization-wide expectation of civil interactions defines the norm for everyone, regardless of stature. Setting expectations also establishes a baseline against which organizations can measure and correct behavior.

Many firms have mission statements, declarations of values, or credos. The following corporate examples clearly emphasize civility, no matter who hears them:

"Treat each other with respect" (from Boeing's integrity statement).

"Above all, employees will be provided the same concern, respect, and caring attitude within the organization that they are expected to share externally with every Southwest Customer" (from Southwest Airlines' mission statement).

"We are responsible to our employees . . . We must respect their dignity" (from the Johnson & Johnson credo).

"FedEx, from its inception, has put its people first both because it is right to do so, and because it is good business as well" (from the opening pages of FedEx's training guide).

"At all times customers and employees are to be treated with dignity and people at all levels should be appreciated and recognized" (from The Limited retail clothing company's operating principles).

"Treat everyone in our diverse community with respect and dignity" (from the mission statement of the Mayo Clinic).

"Foster dignity and respect in all interactions" (Allstate's employment contract).

"Nike was founded on a handshake. Implicit in that act was the determination that we would build our business based on trust, teamwork, honesty and mutual respect" (from Nike's Responsibility Governance statement, which is reviewed and endorsed by signature annually by every Nike employee. It is also applied explicitly to suppliers and contractors who manufacture Nike-branded merchandise).

2. LOOK IN THE MIRROR

Once norms have been set, managers and executives must strive to live by them. Remember that as individuals ascend in an organization, they hear less and less negative information, including information about their own incivility. Think of icons of incivility like Gordon Gecko (brought to life by Michael Douglas in *Wall Street*) or Katharine Parker (played by Sigourney Weaver in *Working Girl*). If their words or deeds offended you or your colleagues, would *you* be complaining to them? Typical employees won't stand up to raw power. Even when given the opportunity for anonymous 360-degree feedback, many people tell us that they are still afraid to speak the truth if the culture is uncivil. They believe that bosses will find a way to figure out who said what and that could put them on the boss's bad side, a precarious positioning, especially if the boss is uncivil. This makes it incumbent on the boss to start improving civility by looking in the mirror.

Begin by evaluating your own actions. It's easy to generate fundamental questions: Do I behave respectfully to all employees? Do I treat individuals on whom I rely, or who can do good things for me, *better* than others? (The answer here, by the way, should be no.) Do I keep a steady temper regardless of the pressures I'm facing? Do I take out my frustrations on employees who have less power than I do? Do I assume that I am omnipotent?

First clue that your boss is a credit hog.

The next step is to have an honest discussion in the C-suite. Peer-to-peer candor can help you become aware of how you're treating one another as well as how you're seen treating subordinates, suppliers, and others. Try videotaping your meetings and conversations. If this sounds like a difficult way to gather information, hire a competent consultant to shadow you and other senior managers, to talk with your subordinates, to give you straight-up feedback, and, if necessary, to teach you the skills you need to become more civil.

Don't assume that you have an accurate reading of your civility. We've heard from company owners, CEOs, corporate presidents, and other senior executives who were astounded to watch themselves during videotaped meetings. As a CEO of a medical firm told us, "I didn't realize what a jerk I sounded like." To his credit, he used the insight well and began to fashion more civil communication.

We love the example of feedback and personal improvement shared by consulting guru Marshall Goldsmith in his book *What Got You Here Won't Get You There*. Goldsmith learned from his own 360-degree evaluation that he had a habit of making destructive comments about his employees behind their backs. He felt terrible, so he vowed to his staff that he was going to change. As motivation, he promised ten dollars to anyone who caught him bad-mouthing the staff. He thought he'd have to plead with employees to get their help, but he soon found that they were happy to oblige. Some even goaded Goldsmith into making such comments. By noon the first day he was down fifty dollars, so he locked himself in his office to spare his wallet. The method worked very quickly. Each day his behavior improved. He spent only thirty dollars the next day, ten the day after that. Before long he had broken his uncivil habit.

3. WEED OUT TROUBLE BEFORE IT ENTERS YOUR ORGANIZATION

The easiest way to foster civility is not to let uncivil people in the door. Not vendors, not contractors, not customers, not employees. Sound impossible? We have some specific suggestions that we've seen work.

Allowing customers to treat your employees badly fosters incivility and puts needless strain on your frontline workers. To assure civility, some firms screen their clients as rigidly as they do their own employees. These aren't just extraordinary firms that dominate their industries, like low-cost competitor Southwest Airlines, but also mid-scale info tech service providers, educational institutions, and retailers. How do they do it? They teach their customers their expectations for respect. If customers' behavior doesn't measure up, they're given fair warning. Then, if customers are still uncivil, these organizations refuse to provide service to them. Southwest is an impressive example. Become belligerent with a flight attendant, and the captain may turn the plane around.

A high-tech firm in Silicon Valley that we know well boasts about "firing" its uncivil clients. Talk to its techs as if you own them, and the company will refuse your business. The owners believe that this stance helps them hire and retain the best and the brightest, making the firm's services even more desirable and improving its ability to turn down detrimental clients.

When it comes to weeding out unfit employees, Jim Collins uses an apt metaphor in his business best seller *Good to Great*. Get the right people on the bus, he urges, and the wrong people off it, and only then figure out where to drive it. Collins's notable examples include Wells Fargo, Walgreens, and Kimberly-Clark. We'd add Southwest Airlines, if just for the motto made famous by founder Herb Kelleher: "Hire for attitude, train for skills."

Savvy sports coaches select players in or out of their teams for civility and respect. Legendary UCLA basketball coach John Wooden honed a knack for weeding out trouble before it could contaminate his Bruins. For Wooden, holding members to high ideals and maintaining exceptional standards of selection were the leader's responsibility. Using his analogy, it meant keeping a rotting apple out of a barrel of good ones. Even before signing a recruit, Wooden relied on his own set of references, not only the recruit's high school coach and teammates but his pastor, the administrators and teachers at his high school, and coaches of opposing teams. Wooden even gathered opinions from some of the opposing teams' players. This effort to weed out uncivil players worked especially well for Wooden because he held himself to no lesser standards. "A coach," he said, "is someone who can give correction without causing resentment."[1]

Do thorough reference checks to weed out problem individuals. Here's another convincing statistic: More than one-third of all job seekers put false information on their résumés and applications. Just because Sean looks like a dream on paper does not mean you should select him. If you care about incivility, you have to dig deeper. Incivility leaves trails. Colleagues know repeat offenders. Uncivil people build bad reputations that extend well beyond their own departments. Sometimes their nasty style is known throughout their industry. Here's another statistic: Despite the availability of information, one-third of organizations do not perform background checks of any kind.

Even in companies that do investigate, efforts are usually not very thorough. Many firms limit their research to the candidate's list of contacts rather than tap personal networks. Other problems can arise when companies use professional search firms. Usually the search firm identifies candidates *and* runs background checks. The problem of course is that a search firm has a vested interest in completing the process. Even if its intentions are good, its efforts may be less than rigorous. Search firms often turn to the same contacts for recommendations as for references. We've heard stories of executive-level offenders who were hired with glowing references. Probing deeper, we've often learned that the search firm that found the new leader also performed her background check.

Even in medicine, where hiring errors can be life-threatening, due diligence may be lacking. At the extreme, consider the incredible story of Michael Swango. His ability to prey on people's trust garnered him admission to medical schools, numerous medical residencies, and a variety of paramedic positions, despite a trail of incarcerations for poisoning people. In his book *Blind Eye*, Pulitzer Prize–winning journalist James B. Stewart tracks the egregious errors made by institutions that hired Swango without careful background checks. At least thirty-five people across the United States and in Africa were murdered by Swango, paying the highest price because organizations they affiliated with had not weeded out trouble before it entered.

It's unlikely that your organization will ever face such devastation because you've let in the wrong people. But Swango's shocking biography just might compel you to think again about allowing people entry into your organization on the basis of "gut" sense or out of desperation.

4. TEACH CIVILITY

Despite broad popular attention to incivility, we're always amazed at how many managers, employees, and professionals tell us that they just don't understand what it means to be civil. They're uncivil by default rather than design. A fourth of the offenders we've interviewed and surveyed claim that they behave uncivilly because they don't know any better. No one at their workplaces has trained them to be respectful of their colleagues, and they have never been shown how rudeness between employees hurts business. For these individuals, training can make a difference.

Lots of training programs are information-based, so employees have gotten used to learning through lectures or by studying notebooks. Yet civility is best learned experientially. Civil demeanor is enhanced by building competencies in such skills as listening, conflict resolution, negotiation, dealing with difficult people, and stress management. Role-playing works well, and it is often enhanced by candid discussion and videotaping.

Training in coaching can boost employees' abilities to help one another when incivility occurs. Knowing how to observe others' behaviors, how to listen for signals that help is needed, how to give and receive feedback, and how to recognize the impact of your own behavior can be invaluable. If your organization already trains managers in coaching, we suggest that you include practice scenarios that focus on employees who have experienced or witnessed incivility.

As with any training efforts, getting people to learn and practice civility requires that companies put in place a formal structure. Civil behavior should be evaluated in performance reviews and tied to career advancement. If you still doubt the importance of training for civility, here's another statistic: Over the years, when we've asked offenders why they're uncivil, one in four blames his bad behavior on lack of training. He claims that he simply doesn't know how to behave and faults his organization for that.

We know of firms that send their doctors to charm school, their attorneys to anger management classes, and their salespeople to negotiation courses. But does priming employees to behave civilly really matter? In a simple experiment conducted by Professor John Bargh and colleagues at New York University, participants were asked to unscramble words. Without their knowledge, their subsequent behaviors were evaluated.[2] In one group the scrambled words related to politeness; in the other, the words related to rudeness. Researchers found that the participants' behavior following the completion of the word test was predictably polite or rude depending on the priming that they had experienced by completing the word tests. People who unscrambled "polite" words were polite; people who unscrambled "rude" words were rude. Priming employees to behave civilly can make a difference. Explaining the distinctions between civil and uncivil behavior is the first step; putting employees through experiential activities to practice civility in action solidifies the change.

5. TRAIN EMPLOYEES AND MANAGERS HOW TO RECOGNIZE AND RESPOND TO SIGNALS

Cunning offenders tend to elude detection, at least for a while. They are often savvy about when, where, and in front of whom they are uncivil, and by targeting less powerful people, they count on their bad behavior going unreported. A fifth of all the offenders we've worked with told us that neither their bosses nor their companies seem to care how employees treat one another. A self-confessed offender told us, "If no one cares, why should I make the extra effort?" For all these reasons, employees and managers need to learn how to spot incivility and how to respond, whether the incivility has been reported or not.

In a hospital we've worked with, doctors are to remain alert to whether staff refuses to work with particular doctors, whether complaints about nurses are circulating through the grapevine, and whether residents seem to be trying to steer clear of certain "mentors." The hospital realizes that nurses, staff, and residents will be reluctant to report bad behavior by senior physicians or if really pushed too far for too long, they will do so as a group, possibly threatening a lawsuit. Therefore the hospital empowers and requires the doctors themselves to monitor their colleagues' behavior. If doctors neglect this responsibility, the hospital holds them personally responsible for the consequences.

6. PUT YOUR EAR TO THE GROUND AND LISTEN CAREFULLY

Three-hundred-sixty-degree feedback can be a powerful tool for curtailing incivility. When feedback is gathered anonymously about an uncivil employee's behavior from subordinates, peers, and superiors, a multidimensional image of the individual develops. Objective organizational data sharpen the picture. Relevant data might include absentee and turnover rates among subordinates or across divisions. These numbers must be interpreted carefully, factoring in such contextual information as current trends among job incumbents, geographic regions of operation, and industry standards, as well as the reasons for absenteeism and turnover. According to executives we have spoken with who have put such analysis into practice, the combination of 360-degree feedback and organizational data is extremely helpful in uncovering weaknesses and strengths.

If we stress the importance of collecting feedback from above, across, and below, this is because offenders tend to present different personas to different hierarchical levels—the "kiss up, kick down" syndrome. If 360-degree feedback is collected carefully, evidence of this pattern will emerge. Remember, respondents must believe that their answers will remain anonymous and that improvements will come as a result of their honesty.

7. WHEN INCIVILITY OCCURS, HAMMER IT

If you ignore incivility, it festers. If offenders get away with it, the behavior is reinforced and repeated, maybe toward their original targets, maybe toward others, maybe toward you. Witnesses who see their colleagues get away with incivility without repercussions may mimic what they see. And if the offender has power, the patterns are strengthened.

A former entertainment executive, whom we'll call Zarger, described his encounters with an Oscar-nominated director-producer. "In the filming of one of his recent releases, he strolled through a warehouse full of extras, publicly admonishing crew members." Zarger added that "it didn't take long before the third assistant director learned from the diatribe and mimicked the behavior on the layer below him." Soon even lower-level crew members openly referred to the extras as nothing but props that eat.

Many managers complain that their colleagues fail to fire habitual offenders. Instead they permit, encourage, or finagle the offenders' transfers to other departments. Some managers and executives tell us that they won't even consider hiring internally anymore because they've been burned by the handoff. What's worse, in many organizations, internal candidates don't have probationary periods. Even if the internal hires' rudeness surfaces right away, it's very difficult to get rid of them quickly.

But restaurateur Danny Meyer believes there's no other choice. Considered the Zagat guide's reigning king for his Manhattan culinary empire, Meyer preaches civility and tolerates nothing less. When someone in one of his eleven restaurants displays a bad attitude, the boss tracks down what happened and tries to help the employee learn from it. If the behavior doesn't change, the employee doesn't stay. It's that simple. As Meyer puts it, he wants his team members to feel "jazzed" about coming to work, and that requires civility without exception.[3]

It's also essential to curtail incivility at the level where many organizations have primary contact with their customers. At Disney disrespectful employees are dismissed quickly. A former Disneyland food cart vendor described the rare occasion when a "cast member" (employee) had upset a "guest" (customer): "No excuses. No second chances. In the three summers that I worked there, I saw it only two or three times, but suits [security, dressed in business attire] descended out of nowhere right away, and then the guy was gone. It hits you pretty hard, and you know they're not kidding with their strict guidelines about how employees are supposed to talk and act with guests."

8. TAKE COMPLAINTS SERIOUSLY

When we've asked employees about incivility, whether through interviews, surveys, focus groups, or on-site consulting, we've never had any difficulty learning which individuals are habitually rude and how. Never. There's a wealth of information about incivility just waiting to be tapped, if complaints are taken seriously. Knowing that employees are generally reluctant to bring forth bad news, savvy leaders work to establish an open door policy and to keep open minds when they hear reports of uncivil interactions. When information surfaces, these leaders know better than to blame the messengers. As an information services worker told us, leaders need to "recognize that it takes a great deal of courage for a lesser-powered employee to report a problem; they fear not being taken seriously or being made to feel like they're the ones committing the act." When exemplary leaders hear about incivility among employees, they gather data quickly, sort out the facts, and take action swiftly, as warranted.

9. DON'T MAKE EXCUSES FOR POWERFUL INSTIGATORS

When we talk to executives about habitual offenders, we hear lots of excuses. Here are a few of the more common ones:

- "That's just how Daryl is."
- "We can't afford to lose Daryl."
- "We're dealing with Daryl but bringing him around in his own time [in his own way, in his own style . . .]. That is the best approach."
- "I don't like to get involved in employees' personal matters."
- "Daryl doesn't really mean any harm. He's just _____." Fill in

the blank: overworked, under a lot of stress, short-tempered, smarter than his colleagues, having problems at home, having problems with his kids, etc.

- "If we try to correct Daryl, he might do something worse."
- "What's the big deal? The complainers need to quit whining."
- "I'm not willing to risk guaranteed income by replacing Daryl."
- "I have bigger problems to focus on elsewhere."
- "It's easier to keep Daryl than to find his replacement."
- "I'm not going to waste my time monitoring trivial problems."
- "Managing 'personal' issues is not my job."
- "We need to help Daryl by being patient and letting him work his problems out on their own."
- "Daryl comes from another country [/culture/generation]. That's how people are there."
- "If you just leave Daryl alone, he's really not all that bad."
- "That's really an HR issue. I don't get involved in those."

The problem with all these excuses (and there are many more!) is that they usually prevent leaders from taking meaningful action. Rather than confront offenders, leaders opt for an easier compromise: They move Daryl to a new location. The unintended consequence is predictable: Daryl continues his uncivil behavior in his new setting. Like a virus, incivility starts infesting another area of the organization.

How do the Daryls of the work world convince their bosses to make excuses for them? Some create the impression that they possess exceptional talent. Others protect themselves by making threats. For their part, some leaders fear confrontation, while others will do their best to avoid "personal" issues, and some simply refuse to go against hierarchical custom. A long-term target of her boss's incivility described it this way: "She would degrade employees and belittle them in front of customers. . . . I am a 'go get 'em' kind of gal, and working for this woman, well, I allowed her to make me feel like I was a child at forty-five because of the way I was treated. When I talked with my district manager, he said, 'When it comes to supporting my managers [meaning the uncivil offender], I will do that before anything.' So I had no choice but to stay quiet, because I knew after that comment it was either 'tattle or take it.'. . . No one would say a word because they did not want to lose their jobs; they too took it. Sad but true. One day I hit my limit, I could not take it anymore, so I quit."

Offenders' bosses do sometimes stand up to incivility. In some cases, there's irrefutable evidence, like pending legal action. More often the manager who stands up to uncivil people believes that incivility is wrong, even when it's coming from exceptionally talented contributors. For one health care executive, documentation was a big help. Files on the offender's "episodes" became the foundation of a full review by a committee of his peers. Once the protective shell began to crack, subordinates lodged their own complaints, prompting the offender to curtail his rudeness and enter an anger management program. The director was proud of having taken action. "The hissy fits ceased, he no longer insulted people, and he no longer threw his feet up on the desk in others' offices. He doesn't speak to me now, but that's okay . . . his behavior is completely different."

It's never easy to take a stand against a powerful offender. Yet the high cost of cutting loose habitually uncivil employees is always outweighed by the outrageous price of keeping them.

10. INVEST IN POSTDEPARTURE INTERVIEWS

Organizational memory fades quickly during the period between an uncivil offense and the target's exit. It's crucial therefore to gather information and reflect upon the experiences and reactions of employees who leave because of incivility. If during their departure interviews you ask targets why they're leaving, the answers you'll get are usually politically correct ones, like "a better offer elsewhere." At this transition point, the target is escaping the uncivil environment; she may still see the offender as threatening and the organization as conspirator. Why should she risk her future?

One way to track the incivility's impact is to conduct *post*departure interviews. There is rich potential in talking with former employees after they've distanced themselves from the organization and settled into their new work environments. Top HR executives have remarked that if they suspect incivility as a cause of departure, they wait about six months after the employee has left and then follow up to gather more information. Sometimes employees who were unwilling to talk about how they were being treated open up. What the HR personnel hear is often quite different from what they were told when the employee left.

When we present this recommendation to our audiences, some people in attendance take exception. They generally agree that collecting data postdeparture sounds good in theory, but they find it less useful in practice. What we've learned from them is that if the industry involved is too small or if the offender is too powerful, targets will still fear that coming forward will ruin their careers. "Why should targets tell the truth after leaving the organization," we're asked, "when they wouldn't even speak up from inside?" We still contend that postdeparture interviews hold promise. They're relatively inexpensive, and often they do pay off. Sometimes the new environment gives targets clearer insight into their former experiences with incivility, and that makes them ready to share those insights.

There you have it, a short list of relatively small actions that can lead to big differences. If you want your organization to reap the payoffs of civil behavior, start by setting expectations and making sure that your own behavior lines up well. Be sure everyone in your organization knows what's expected of him or her. For heaven's sake, don't let in people you think will cross that line; there's too much at stake, including the welfare of your organization. Keep on the lookout for uncivil words and deeds, and listen when people complain about them. Once they're spotted, do something to correct and curtail them. Demonstrate that you mean business when it comes to assuring civil, respectful interaction.

Addressing incivility makes a difference. Getting started is not easy, but even small successes can activate a flywheel moving toward mutual respect and civility. Taking incremental steps that we have outlined here could affect fundamental changes in individual firms and across the business world as a whole.

14

What's a Leader to Do?

Nearly all men can stand adversity, but if you want to test a man's character, give him power.

—Abraham Lincoln

UNDERSTANDING RECOMMENDATIONS is easy; it's far more difficult to put them into practice. Consistency and perseverance are key, and that means devoting time and attention, two resources in short supply, especially for managers and leaders. In addition to listening, watching, and probing for warning signals of bad behavior, leaders need to act on those signals. We're switching to a question-and-answer format here, providing our responses to issues that have been raised by managers and executives we've worked with over the years.

Around my company I reward toughness. We demand more from less; it's part of our culture. We're driven and proud of it. We recruit, select, and motivate for extreme competition. Seems like being nice is for powder puff organizations, maybe for the HR department, but not us.

We've got more than a decade's worth of data that says you're mistaken in believing that there's any business organization out there that would not improve with increased civility. Civility isn't about "being nice"; it's about working with mutual respect. It's not the stuff of tea parties; it's about working hard, working tough, getting the most that you can out of your employees. Add more civility to the mix and you'll find greater payoffs, including increased loyalty to the company and to you.

I'm pretty sure I'm civil with people who work here with me, but we're expanding globally. With my next promotion, I'll have people reporting to me from all over the world. How can I best safeguard civility?

Going global raises two challenges when it comes to civility: distance and cross-cultural norms. We've worked with hundreds of teams that must manage their effectiveness at a distance, complete with time zone differences, asynchronous communication formats, cultural value disparities, and other media and human relations challenges. Top on our list of recommendations is to bring distanced people together in person so that they can "read" each other and develop rapport face-to-face, even if only for a few days each year. The focus of the meeting is almost immaterial, so long as it provides gently facilitated opportunities for getting acquainted casually. As for the cross-cultural challenges, learn how fundamental values differ between your culture and those that you will be leading. There are many sources to consult about this, and they are always broadly generalized, as they must be; but they provide a starting place from which you can adjust the stereotypes as your experiences and observations grow. An excellent reference that succinctly describes practical value differences across more than a hundred cultures is *Kiss, Bow or Shake Hands*. Greater detail about cultural differences and how they affect business relationships can also be found on the Internet, including the GLOBE study (*Culture, Leadership, and Organizations* by Bob House and colleagues) and the Cultural Orientations Indicator (www.culturalnavigator.com).

Okay, let's say you've convinced me that it pays to be civil. My concern is that others in my company will think I've lost my edge, that I've gone soft, that my newfound concern for how employees treat one another is just plain silly.

Ask for five minutes of their time. Brief them quickly on what incivility is, how it can fall between the cracks, and how dissatisfied most employees are with the way their companies manage it. Tell your colleagues how offenders are as opportunistic as Eddie Haskell when it comes to choosing their targets and their timing. Then bring in a few numbers, like how often people experience or witness incivility at work, how many leave, how many get back at their offenders and at their organizations. Make it a quick conversation. Then ask your colleagues to help you estimate how much these outcomes of incivility could be costing *your* company. Do you think they'll still think you're soft?

Is there really never *a time when it's appropriate to be uncivil?*

Right. Never. We'll say this again, without qualification: Civility is more effective than incivility. Even when the world seems to be crashing around you. Perhaps especially then. An executive we confer with pushed us on this. As a pilot he was adamant that the tragic crash of Air Florida Flight 90 (see Chapter 8) could have been avoided if the copilot had taken control, if he had done something, anything to grab the pilot's attention, even if it required screaming or cursing at the pilot. The problem is that disrespectful behavior requires the target to listen through and beyond the disrespect, and that's challenging for anyone, especially in times of crisis. Our data confirm that targets will struggle to concentrate when treated badly. They'll lose focus trying to understand the incivility and how to respond. And don't forget the emotional impact, which further distracts and short-circuits their ability to be effective. Incivility doesn't shock people into better focus. It robs concentration, hijacks task orientation, and impedes performance. Greater assertiveness may have been called for in the tragic case of Flight 90; but disrespect was not the answer then, and it is never the answer.

It sounds good to demand civility among our employees, but can you point to some leaders who have actually succeeded by doing this?

Two gems come right to mind: Jim Sinegal at Costco and Isadore Sharp at Four Seasons. For Sinegal, customers and employees are more important than stockholders, and he makes sure that Costco lives by that value, whether measured in pay, benefits, or promotions. A positive, civil environment and good benefits allow Costco to hire better people who stay longer and are more efficient than in other warehouse operations. Sinegal walks the talk too, drawing a salary of only $350,000 (2005) from a $60-plus billion business. And there's a bonus for treating employees right: Costco does no general advertising. As Sinegal has said, "Imagine that you have 120,000 loyal ambassadors out there who are constantly saying good things about Costco. It has to be a significant advantage for you."[1]

The Four Seasons luxury hotels have been on *Fortune*'s list of the Best Companies to Work For since 1998, the first year this list was compiled. Guests willingly drop thousands of dollars per night for special pampering by Four Seasons employees. What draws these extraordinary employees? Founder/Chairman/CEO Isadore Sharp credits a twist on the Golden Rule: "How you treat your employees is how you expect them to treat the customer."[2] In exchange for embracing company values, employees themselves are pampered. They get free stays in any of the hotels, and during their visits they're treated like guests, not freebies. What's the payoff for this kind of employee respect? Turnover is less than 20 percent annually, about half the industry average. Recruiting is no problem either. Last year, to staff the new Qatar property, forty-two applicants showed up for every job opening. Recently *Fortune* described the demeanor of a leader within Four Seasons, a general manager/regional vice president who helps set the course for civility. The article noted how he regularly listens to his employees, remedies problems without holding grudges, and deflects any credit that may flow his way. In short, he's civil.[3]

We're about to appoint a new senior executive. It's pretty tough to pick up on incivility in interviews, let alone a résumé. Any suggestions?

We have several recommendations:

- Let all candidates know how important mutual respect is in your organization, that you do not tolerate incivility. Back this up with real examples about offenders in your company. If you're persuasive (and lucky), would-be offenders will back out of the running on this information alone.

- Ask for specific examples of their past behaviors when you interview candidates. Get them to support their appealing descriptions of civil behavior with past actions that they actually took.
- Talk to people at lower levels who have worked with the candidate (think "kiss up, kick down").
- Use a team approach. If someone on the recruiting team gets a bad vibe, pursue it. Time invested could save you a sour hire.
- Check references. Check references. Check references.
- If you spot a problem, keep searching.

Our company tends to promote from within, but one of the rudest people here came with a glowing recommendation from her boss in another division. How can we avoid making that mistake again?

Approach each candidate with measured cynicism. Tap internal networks that you and your colleagues have worked so hard to build. Use those contacts to get a full profile of the candidate—across levels, across divisions, across functions.

We have an uncivil power elite group in our organization. They're high-performing professionals and well aware of it. Our top executives cave in to their demands for fear of losing anyone in the group. They're blatantly rude and demanding of people at all levels, including senior executives. What can we do?

Changes needed here have to come from the top. Until the senior executives recognize that condoning incivility—even from "stars"—is costing the organization dearly, things are unlikely to change. If they're peers, you could put your career at risk by trying to bring their incivilities to executive attention. And without some changes from above, the likelihood of long-term change is probably pretty dismal.

When it comes to incivility, there's power in numbers. When there's a power elite clique, some of their power is derived simply from their ability to stand as a team. When this happens, potential targets have to "watch their backs" from many angles. Even if you're of equal power, if you try to take on an uncivil member of the clique, it may bring her comrades rushing to the rescue, especially if they believe that the force of the group is at stake. However, if you're in a power position, looking down (hierarchically) at the clique, you have an opportunity and responsibility to read on.

Suppose I've had enough incivility from the power elite clique and I'm sitting in a higher position. What can I do?

Calling a powerful clique to task can take nerves of steel, even for senior executives. Make sure your own behavior is civil. Then be sure that you are clearly communicating your expectations for civil, respectful interactions from *all* members of the organization. Give the entire organization notice about the nature of the repercussions that will be incurred by repeat offenders. Use multiple communication approaches (e.g., presentations, additions to the corporate credo, small group meetings flowing down the hierarchy) so that you can rest assured that everyone has heard the message. Once it has been communicated, trounce episodes of repeated incivility. No flinching for offenders' power, experience, or special skills. As soon as offenders understand that there really is no immunity, their behaviors will improve. If their behaviors don't improve, reexamine the consequences, and make sure that the costs of incivility are sufficiently averse.

Sometimes eliminating a key member of the clique will be enough to bring the others in line. At a technology firm we worked with, employees were so used to being treated badly by a power clique that they quit reporting offenses. Luckily for them, their VP boss realized that something was wrong. Too many good people were leaving. When he investigated, he learned that some of his best and brightest had left because they were fed up with the incivilities of the power elite clique. Over time the clique had intimidated people into giving them the best jobs, the best opportunities, the best perks. Some got corner offices ahead of their due. Others traveled to the most desirable locations on assignment. Some jumped promotion levels without merit. Three members of the clique had unruly tempers and had exploded several times at lower-level employees. But it took a large meeting during which the clique's chief offender blew up at the president before things turned around. This perpetrator was called to task, warned that he'd lose his prestigious title if he didn't treat people right. Almost as if by a miracle, the whole clique's uncivil behavior subsided.

What's the best way to learn more about civility, and how can we help others in our organization do the same?

If you still harbor any reluctance to take on the challenges of curtailing incivility, find an adviser, a coach, a consultant. Look for someone you trust, a great observer who will give you honest answers and ask tough questions. You might also do additional reading, maybe circulate some good books around your organization. We hope you'll include this one, and we have further recommendations. If you're looking for a broad overview of what civility is all about, why it's important, and what's needed to achieve it, we suggest *Choose Civility* by P. M. Forni. It's a quick and solid read, full of practical advice about practicing civility in our daily lives. Bob Sutton's *No Asshole Rule* adds first-rate advice about how and why you should keep offenders out of your workplace.

We've also found great TV episodes and films portraying civility. Drive home the escalation of incivility with a lot of humor in "High Crane Drifter," a classic episode of *Frasier* that we mentioned earlier. Our top nominee for the all-time icon of civility is Henry Fonda as the architect in *12 Angry Men*. Listen and watch as he unleashes the power of civility to move an entire jury, one by one. If you'd prefer movies focused on our connectedness and the power of civility, watch *Six Degrees of Separation*, *Crash*, or *Babel*. Share favorites with your employees; movies can turn a training session into a treat, and if you can capture participants' attention, they'll be far more likely to remember the message.

We hope the variety of approaches that we've described here and in Chapter 13 help you recognize that there's not just one right way to assure civility. You'll succeed by adopting and tailoring approaches fit for your organization so long as you establish a baseline, compare that with the desired future, and start taking steps to close the gap. As you've seen, sometimes those steps are easy to do (like informing employees that you expect them to treat one another with mutual respect), and sometimes those steps are challenging (like accepting nothing less, no matter who the offender is). The important thing is to get started, stay mindful, and keep improving.

15

What's a Target to Do?

If you're going through hell, keep going.

—Winston Churchill

How should targets deal with their offenders? How should they protect themselves? How can they best cope? In this chapter we address targets who find themselves in precarious situations in which their offenders hold as much as or more power than they do. If you're being targeted by an offender who has less power than you do, then Chapter 14's tips for top-down situations apply.

Fighting back when the offender has more power requires courage, and it can cost the lesser-powered targets promotions, opportunities, and even jobs. We believe that it is our responsibility to begin this chapter by warning against some popular advice. Unfortunately, there are people who write, lecture, and advise about incivility and bullying by comparing the workplace with the playground. They recommend that targets fight back, treating offenders as if they were schoolyard bullies. We have more than a decade of research that says this guidance is dangerous.

Workplace offenders have very little in common with schoolyard bullies. Two-thirds of workplace offenders have the power of the organizational hierarchy behind them; they call the shots on the corporate playing field. Although some high-power organizational offenders may seem at first to accept your push back, you must not forget that they have resources, connections, and hierarchical perspective that exceed your own. That would mean, in the playground analogy, that the principal and the teachers would be the bullies.

Additionally, the school playground is monitored. A teacher or some other responsible adult capable of overpowering bullies makes sure that peace prevails. Few organizations have powerful individuals who are looking out for incivility or who are trained to deal with it effectively if they spot it. Treating offenders in the workplace as if they were schoolyard bullies can be (work)life-threatening when they have greater power than you do. Do not confront your offender under these circumstances, even if that individual is not your direct boss.

We're not suggesting that you sit idly by and do nothing. Stewing about incivility can cause greater insecurity, lower self-esteem, and increased sense of helplessness. It can undermine your performance while your focus is drawn away from the tasks at hand. We recommend action over inaction, and we want to tell you about many specific approaches that have worked for targets of lesser or equal power as their offenders. We have filtered these eight recommendations through our own observations and expertise and those of colleagues schooled in law, psychology, and human resources.

RECOGNIZE THE PERSONAL TOLL

It hurts to be demeaned, disregarded, or disrespected, regardless of your status, self-confidence, or personal strength. When you're the target of incivility, it's common to lose trust in individuals and in institutions and to feel nervous, stressed, or tense. If your job security feels threatened, your routine is disrupted dramatically (e.g., lack of sleep), or you suffer losses in status or personal friendships, the negative impact can be emotional, physiological, behavioral, or any combination of these.

So do yourself a favor: Recognize that your workplace effectiveness is likely to drop. If you've been the target of incivility, it's time to pay special attention to taking care of yourself. Surround yourself with friends and family members who build you back up. Make time for relaxation and fun. Schedule downtime when you can get away completely from work strains. You might even collect some positive feedback from people whose opinions you value. A *Harvard Business Review* article titled "How to Play to Your Strengths" can help you with the rationale and practical guidance for getting started.[1] Exercise more; eat right; indulge in simple pleasures that matter to you. All these actions can help you compensate for incivility's depleting effects.

APPEAL TO A HIGHER AUTHORITY

Virtually all targets appeal to someone, whether family, friends, or colleagues. But very few appeal to anyone who has the power to stop the incivility. If you want to put an end to the bad behavior, you must find an advocate who has the organizational power to address incivility head-on. For some of you, this could be a manager or executive who outranks your offender; for others, it could be a human resources or employee assistance specialist whose expertise, responsibility, and authority match the need.

Sadly, some targets tell us that taking problems up to higher levels is impossible in their organizations. They say that people sitting atop their firms are inaccessible or that they (the leaders) lack conviction or courage. If this applies in your workplace, you might try teaching powerful allies how it costs to be uncivil. Working the issue of incivility upward is most successful if you prepare carefully and provide succinct explanations about why organizations should care. For executives, showing cost savings can go a long way. This book is full of examples that we hope will be useful.

If your efforts to appeal upward at work are thwarted, you may want to turn to an even higher power. Some targets pray or confer with religious leaders. Others read the Bible, the Koran, the Torah, or the writings of scholars and prophets. For expanding personal perspectives positively, you might also try *The Analects* of Confucius, *The Art of Happiness* by the Dalai Lama, *The Art of Possibility* by Rosamund and Benjamin Zander, or *The Dream Manager* by Matthew Kelly.

When trampled by mistreatment, many people tell us that they find comfort in applying the Golden Rule. Caroline described an episode in which she was the target of incivility from a newcomer in her department: "I guess she was trying to impress everyone with how much she knew. But in doing so she set about disparaging me and setting folks against me. She spread negative rumors about me and belittled my opinion." At first Caroline wanted to get even, but she considered the ramifications her reactions could have. "I decided to safeguard my positive image. Rather than look for ways to get even, I would treat her the way I like to be treated. I wanted harmony, so I followed my own set of values."

BACK OFF

There are lots of ways to retreat and recoil from an offender. You can reduce your dependence on your ill-mannered colleague by seeking advice, information, and support from peers or bosses. You can become more proactive and independent in accomplishing your tasks, conferring with the offender only when absolutely necessary. You can also strategically reduce your offender's dependence on you by diverting his or her less important requests to other employees. Taking charge of your life at work is challenging. A phenomenal starting place is with a philosophical reevaluation of your personal (and likely insatiable?) quest for getting ahead. We know of no better book to get you started than *Status Anxiety* by Swiss philosopher Alain de Botton. This entertaining resource might just help you topple your fears about where you stand at work and far beyond.

Anna, an information technology specialist who was known throughout her company for her helpful can-do attitude, was tired of being taken for granted and having her contributions ignored by her boss and others who turned to her. "I started looking at how much [my boss] relied on me and how I was always there with the answer, even before he asked the question. I didn't feel like my efforts were appreciated. He never said 'please' or 'thank you,' and when things weren't going well, he acted like it was my fault." Anna was getting burned out, so she started cutting back, just a little. Now when her boss asked her for help, she directed him to others who could also answer his questions. "I was very pleasant about it. It might have taken him a little longer to get the information he needed; but it didn't seem to have had any really bad effects, and it sure made a lot of difference to me not to always have to be the go-to person."

Targets share many helpful tips for limiting exposure to an uncivil individual. Practical options include:

- Schedule shorter meetings.
- Communicate with the offender via phone or e-mail rather than face-to-face.
- Meet with the offender away from your own office (so that you can control the end of the meeting through your departure), preferably in a neutral setting.
- Stay off committees or teams that include the offender.
- Work different days/shifts from your offender.
- Work from home.
- Do as much as you can through the individual's assistant or partner (if they behave civilly).
- Avoid meeting with the offender alone.

In addition to staying clear of offenders, lots of targets back off from their work environments. You might stop attending optional social occasions (e.g., parties at the boss's house, lunches in the company cafeteria), reduce the amount of extra hours you put in, and start taking those accrued vacation and sick days. You might also stop volunteering to serve on committees or in roles that go beyond your job responsibilities. We do not recommend sloughing off work assignments or putting less than your best effort into your job, as that can lead to a disastrous downward spiral. Still, if cutting back on your extra efforts can make the difference between staying and leaving, it's worth considering.

REFRAME YOUR THINKING

Even if you can't change the offender's behavior, you can change *your* attitude. Some targets redirect their frustration, disappointment, and anger by rising above the incivility. They describe their motivation to "turn the other cheek" or to "show that I have higher character than he does." This change in thinking is not so much spiritually motivated as it is survival or endurance driven. You benefit by taking this perspective because churning about the incivility or the offender is a distraction that impairs your own concentration and performance. If you muster the strength to rise above the negative, you stamp out stress before it harms you.

In one of our studies, we asked targets to tell us the reasons why they reframed their thinking rather than seek some sort of retribution. They shared a wide variety of rationales:

- Protecting my own image: "I was confident in my abilities and judgment. I was cognizant of the impression my reaction would leave."
- No chance of improvement: "He [the offender] is a high-level executive, and everyone knows his behavior patterns. It has happened before and was not unexpected."
- Too risky: "I didn't want to get fired."
- Cosmic justice: "People like this eventually do themselves in, given time and space."
- Company will deal with it: "We don't get even in our organization. It's well stated in our policy manual."
- Apathy toward offender: "She's not worth my time and effort. I feel complete and absolute disregard toward the witch."
- Part of job requirement: "It is my job to work with him. I will continue to do my job. I will, however, never work with him by myself."
- Wrong timing: "I will take action eventually, but for now I'm doing nothing. I have not yet found the opportunity."

In organizations in which incivility has free rein, in which programs to enhance employee involvement and participation seem more like schemes to increase productivity without reciprocal benefits, reframing your thinking can plausibly entail withdrawing emotionally from your job. As Bob Sutton points out in his book *The No Asshole Rule*, "All this talk about passion, commitment and identification with an organization is absolutely correct *if* you are in a good job and are treated with dignity and respect. But it is hypocritical nonsense to the millions of people who are trapped in jobs and companies where they feel oppressed and humiliated. . . ."[2] If you've been treated uncivilly and no one seems to care, you might try just going through the motions, reducing your extraordinary contributions, and putting your heartfelt efforts into your life outside work.

GROW

Incivility presents opportunities for you to grow. Nietzsche had it right when he said, "What doesn't kill me makes me stronger." You might, for instance, take advantage of the uncivil work environment to learn how to work with a jerk, a skill that could be useful throughout your career.

Even JFK Airport's own Web site calls it the airport people love to hate. So imagine our surprise when we learned that five hundred ticket agents, parking attendants, and other front liners at Kennedy are taking civility training. They even go through role plays to improve their diplomacy by learning to "bounce back" and fortify their resiliency. Too bad for them that Kennedy's passengers don't have to take similar courses.

You could grow by reflecting carefully about how the incivility transpired, how it affected you, how you have drawn strength, and how your experience of incivility has changed your thinking or behavior. So-called

New Age books like Marianne Williamson's *The Gift of Change* and Eckhart Tolle's *A New Earth* might improve your ability to see incivility as an opportunity for personal growth and transformation. You might consider asking friends or other colleagues for their interpretations, recommendations for action, and support. Insights they share could restore your spirit, reduce your stress, and help you identify additional contexts or past experiences that may have aggravated or mitigated your reaction to the incivility.

You might look upon the incivility as a cue to reinforce your positive self-image. Professor Jane Dutton, at the University of Michigan, points to the reaffirming effect that appreciative letters, e-mail messages, and artifacts can have when we are treated badly. In *Energize Your Workplace*, Dutton describes how these sources of data help us bolster our self-image and reinforce our positive self-talk. We have found that a file of complimentary e-mail messages from students, a box of inspiring letters from colleagues and mentors, and various trinkets inherited from our strongest ancestors serve as amulets or talismans that help protect us from "evil spirits." Whether or not reinforced by baubles, if you are armed with a positive perspective, you may find yourself better able to cope with incivility. Remember that you have endured and survived. That alone should foster a sense of personal accomplishment.

DECIDE TO STAY PUT

Many targets hang tough. If that's your decision, it is important to recognize that you have made a *choice*. Don't stay because you fear that you have no other options or because you believe that you owe it to your organization. Stay because that is what you have decided to do. Recognize your tenacity to renew your sense of power and self-confidence. Take pride in your resilience and reinforce that by learning more about emotional intelligence from books like Daniel Goleman's original *Emotional Intelligence* or his newer volume, *Working with Emotional Intelligence*. Alternately, hit the topic head-on by reading *The Resilience Factor* by Karen Reivich and Andrew Shatte.

If you decide to stick it out, you might want to make a list of the specific reasons why you are staying. You can learn a lot by documenting your thoughts, and the list might just provide a great baseline to measure against, whether your work environment improves or gets even worse. A senior professional, Ron, provides a solid example: "Some of the people I work with are real jerks; it's not just one guy who's rude around here. But after giving it lots of thought—and I did think about it a lot, too much, probably—I realized that I love my job and I like living in this city and the pay and benefits are excellent. The only big problem is that I have to work with some nasty, self-centered people. Dealing with these egocentrics is challenging, but I decided that I'm not going to let their attitudes push me out of here. When I was complaining to a close friend, he made a recommendation that helps, and I follow it on really crappy days: I just open my desk drawer and take a close look at my latest pay stub." Whether as resilience, determination, or fortitude, the empowering perspective is that you are making a choice.

LEAVE

If you list the pros and cons of staying and leaving, you might find that the balance tips toward exiting. This can be a sound decision under certain circumstances. If you're flooded with offers of better opportunities, incivility could be the "kick in the pants with a golden horseshoe" that gets you moving in a new and better direction. Getting away from an offender or leaving an environment that condones incivility could improve your day-to-day experience and your career. Likewise, if your workplace seems destined to remain uncivil and you're tired of putting in valiant efforts as the self-appointed change master, or if workplace incivilities are compromising your life away from work or destroying your self-image, it could well be time to leave. For those in the rut of accepting workplace incivility, we recommend reading Mary Catherine Bateson's stimulating treatment of the concept of achievement in *Composing a Life*, a book that might just change your attitude toward new beginnings. No one is under any obligation to work with another person whose behavior is demoralizing, upsetting, or stress-inducing. After all, it's just a *job*.

Tom, a vice president of a midsize construction firm, described his response after the president violently chastised him for leaving work for a few minutes. Tom had been with the company for nearly a decade, but after this incident he and the boss began avoiding each other. Tom cut back his work hours, lost time worrying about what was going on, and took out his bad feelings at home. In the end he quit. "I wanted to get even, but I didn't," Tom explained. "So I resigned. I had lost respect for the president, and my performance was lagging. I didn't like the way I was treated, and my confidence was diminishing." There are lots of reasons why escaping incivility makes sense and lots of reasons why it doesn't. It's essential to weigh the pros and cons carefully on the basis of your personal circumstances.

NEGOTIATE WITH THE OFFENDER

There's only one action that should be weighed even more carefully than departure, and that is approaching your higher-level offender about the incivility. We cautiously avoid calling this action confronting the offender or dealing with the offender because it might imply provoking or challenging your offender's behavior with an eye toward gaining an upper hand. Don't provoke, and don't expect to "win." If you're considering a follow-up with your offender, think like a negotiator. Know your limits. Before you even schedule a meeting, prepare. Proceed with the goal of mutual gain.

Dealing with a difficult person is never easy, but some approaches tend to work better than others. Before talking with your offender, consider going through a rehearsal where you test your ideas and style with people who can give you honest feedback. Ask them to role-play the offender, complete with all the tics and temperament that you know. Brush up on your emotional intelligence skills. Competencies like self-awareness and self-regulation will be essential. You might even need to practice empathy toward your offender. Hone your listening skills to their finest. Remember that we listen mostly by observing nonverbal behaviors, so when you're practicing and preparing, focus on reading the offender's physical interaction and regulating your own. Most of us get ready for challenging interactions by thinking precisely about the words we will choose. As decades of communication studies have shown, the actual words carry far less meaning than the way in which they are delivered. Work to control your tone of voice and volume and to remain calm if your offender does not do the same. Give yourself a head start on understanding body language by taking a look at Allan and Barbara Pease's *The Definitive Book of Body Language*.

If you're going to speak with your offender, think very carefully about the setting and whether you will include other people as witnesses or mediators. If your offender is volatile, do not have this meeting in private. It may not be appropriate to include workplace chums, but don't go it alone or you may leave yourself vulnerable to further tirades. A target we know broached her difficult discussion while she and her offender were walking along a busy street on the way back from a meeting. The setting worked well for her. It was away from either person's terrain, and they were surrounded by cars full of witnesses should the offender go ballistic. Whatever your circumstances, plan the big picture before you even approach the offender. Decipher what's at stake and how you'll achieve the best outcome. *Difficult Conversations* by Douglas Stone, Bruce Patton, and Sheila Heen is a good resource for those choosing this risky path.

If you're very lucky, your offender might possibly recognize the error of his ways. Even when this doesn't happen, the fates intervene in other ways. A recently hired financial consultant described a situation she faced involving a higher-ranking male colleague who was not her supervisor: "It started with a couple of e-mails. They were insulting. He accused me of misrepresenting a situation. I was off-site in a training class, so I couldn't do anything right away. Eventually I talked to my boss, a few friends at work, and my husband. I thought about trying to get even with my coworker, but I decided to discuss it calmly with him instead. I knew that I had been strong and my performance actually improved because of that. But after speaking with him, I just stayed away from him. I had already lost any respect for him. I didn't leave. He did. He quit within the year."

Lots of paths available to targets can lead to happy endings. Lean on your support system, learn what you can, and then put your plans into motion. Don't sulk, and don't let the incivility or the offender eat away at your focus, your spirit, or your potential.

In this chapter, we have tried to give targets a portfolio of options for dealing with incivility. The actions we've suggested will lead you to your best self and help you discover what the best environment is for you. Keep in mind that you may need to diverge from your first-choice alternative. You may find it impossible, for instance, to negotiate successfully with your offender; in that case, you might decide to move on, or you might try first to work around your offender or discover that rising above the situation is more effective.

One thing is certain: Dealing with incivility offers an opportunity for growth. Bad as it feels to be treated disrespectfully, you do have options. Paradoxically, the very efforts intended to demean you can help you soar to new levels. The key is to take control and choose your own responses. So do us and yourselves a favor: Follow Winston Churchill's advice, and just keep going!

16

What's an Offender to Do?

If you wouldn't write it and sign it, don't say it.
—Earl Wilson, columnist

IF YOU'RE UNCIVIL by nature, it's unlikely that you would even pick up this book. But if you're occasionally out of line, or if you regret offending once in a while, even if you didn't mean any harm, this chapter is for you. By now you have a clear sense of what incivility could be costing your colleagues, your subordinates, your organization, and even you. You probably don't like the thought of offending others or of people complaining about you. And you certainly wouldn't want your associates dancing in the halls the day that you leave. If you're inclined to improve your civility, read on. People who behave uncivilly, and who care about the problems incivility creates, certainly can change. It all begins with wanting to improve.

START WITH THE BASIC ABCD

Theresa was a small business owner in her forties who had always enjoyed work. She started her management consulting firm alone about six years ago, and one success after another led to expansions. Her top-tier staff now numbers a dozen highly qualified, diligent professionals and support personnel. Clients are delighted by the services they receive, and profits allow Theresa to reward her employees well through strong salaries and solid perks. Business is booming beyond Theresa's blue-sky projections. But she is not happy. She approached us with the following complaint: "I'm an offender. I know it. Nobody at work has told me so, but I know that I say things that are rude. I'm disrespectful to my employees sometimes. It's probably because of pressures I put on myself. They don't complain, but I know I'm not treating them as well as I should, and that makes me unhappy. I didn't used to be like this, and I really want to change."

If you truly want to become more civil and more respectful, you can. One approach is as easy to remember as ABCD. Whether you're going to try to improve through self-study or by working with a coach or coaches, it's vital to identify the Antecedents, what has led to your incivility; the Behaviors, what specific ways you are uncivil; the Consequences, what's reinforcing your bad behavior; and Direction, what you can do about it.

GATHER DATA

There are various ways to study your uncivil behaviors. You can ask people straight out; you can ask them to complete surveys; you can even keep a personal log. You might note behaviors that seemed rude to you, behaviors that seemed to shut other people down, cause them to grimace or walk away from you. You might start with some self-help, but to see the full picture, you must include others' perspectives. It's human nature to see ourselves in a positive light. We forget the slights we dish out very quickly, if we notice them at all. However, our data clearly show that those same slights are remembered in detail—sometimes for years—by the people we've slighted.

If you have not collected 360-degree feedback, this is an ideal starting place.

A senior-level surgeon at a teaching hospital admitted to us that until he received this upward feedback, he had never thought twice about his condescending comments or gestures, although, as our research showed, almost all his residents did. He lamented that he simply couldn't understand why so many residents complained about being treated uncivilly by him. After all, he explained, he wasn't doing anything that he hadn't experienced as a resident. "This kind of training is what we all went through. So, why are all these recent crops of residents so *soft*?" When confronted with the 360-degree feedback data, the surgeon admitted that he made derogatory remarks and conducted himself without any thought of impropriety, and now he was beginning to understand the costs of his behavior.

We recommend videotaping your meetings and other workplace interactions. Capturing diverse encounters candidly can give you a fresh perspective on your strengths and weaknesses. Videotapes help you look at yourself—facial expressions, body posture, words, and tone of voice—as others see you. Managers and executives that we have worked with are sometimes surprised at what they see. As a senior executive confessed, "I was stunned when I watched the tape. I didn't know how easy it was for others to read my responses. I thought I had a poker face, but there were really obvious 'tells.' I'd look away if I didn't like something or if I wasn't particularly interested in what was being discussed. I thought people wouldn't notice, sometimes I wasn't even aware that I was doing it, but it was right there on the tape." While watching videotaped interactions, focus on what you're communicating regarding respect. Which behaviors and words communicate regard for others and which seem rude? Plan to repeat the former and quit doing the latter.

It takes a little while to forget that the camera is there, but once it is forgotten, people do slip into their normal patterns. We know from our own experiences coaching managers that it is very useful to view the videos several times: (1) Watch with sound as an overview, to sense the general demeanor of civility or incivility that you are communicating; (2) watch without sound to focus on nonverbal behaviors, such as facial expressions, gestures, distancing, and movement toward or away from others; and (3) listen with no image so that you can focus on voice tone, volume, and speed of speech, as well as the words you choose.

If you lack that winning smile, Nintendo may have your answer.
Its digital DS camera includes a Face Training game complete with

sixteen exercises to hone your facial muscle control (and enhance your good looks while doing so!). It might turn out to be the next latest, greatest invention for cross-cultural communication. The dual-screen, hand-held player shows animation of perfected "facening" skills on one screen and your own face on the other. Players get immediate feedback to perfect their winks, glares, and smiles, facilitating continuous improvement when it comes to civil/uncivil facial expressions.

FIND A GREAT COACH

Personal coaches help. They can seek candid, detailed, grounded information from individuals who work with you and then use their insights to tailor your feedback. Coaches have an advantage over self-help because they lack self-serving bias regarding you and can gather and apply information without revealing critics' identities. Their experience and expertise can help guide you through the ABCDs, and they can provide more objective feedback based on others' perceptions and more honest feedback because they are not your coworkers. A great coach will help you identify your shortcomings, figure out practical, behavioral improvements, and hold you to them.

DIG DEEPER ON YOUR OWN

Personal reflection is another tool for increasing civility. This self-study can be guided by keeping a log or a journal that suits your personal needs. You might keep track of when/where/why you were less than respectful. You can note examples of civility and incivility that you see around you, and you could create to-do lists of simple changes that you want to make.

Keeping a personal journal can give you insight into when you are your best, most civil self and when you are likely to be out of sorts or uncivil. One offender we've worked with, Monica, noticed that she was far curter in the late afternoon. She began her days at 5:00 A.M. or earlier. By the time late afternoon hit, she was tired, lacked energy, and was less emotionally attuned to herself and to others. She was brusque in conversations and less civil in e-mail. Before keeping a journal, Monica was unaware of the effect of time of day on her demeanor. Now, if she has to attend meetings, participate in conference calls, or work with teammates in the late afternoon, she is much more mindful of her behavior.

Ivan is a professional in an information-driven environment who prides himself on his warm personality and his ability to get along well with almost everyone. People at all levels who work with Ivan and even those who encounter him by chance tend to agree. Colleagues confide in him, and he is often given high-visibility assignments that require tact and an evenhanded approach. Ivan is well liked, respected, a very civil individual. Yet as he learned more about incivility, he became aware of his tendency to disparage a few nasty colleagues behind their backs. "I hadn't thought about it much until I considered the negative role modeling that I was doing. I criticized only people who were obnoxious to others, I shared my criticisms only with people I trusted, and in private, and somehow all that made it seem okay. Then I started thinking about how I was out of line just like the few nasty people around here. It was a real eye-opener, and I decided that I wanted to set a better example." Ivan began by reflecting about his ABCs. He knew that he was very sensitive to injustice toward others (A), especially when it was downward-facing. When he heard about those kinds of demeaning encounters, he spared no details while condemning the offenders in private conversations with his confidants (B). He also realized that those discussions were captivating to listeners. He thought he had strengthened ties with his friends at work at the same time that he was paving a destructive path for the offender (C). But when Ivan began to disentangle the unintended consequences, he realized that his own behavior was uncivil. It wasn't easy for Ivan to change, even when he understood his ABCDs, but he was determined to improve.

Ivan made small but significant changes (D). First, he remained alert to his shortcoming. He kept an index card in his pocket, and when he caught himself criticizing people behind their backs, he made note of the person to whom he was talking, why the conversation had occurred, and what he was thinking at the time. When he heard rumors of mistreatment, he didn't respond by gossiping, but rather created a time lag by jotting down notes about what he knew and what more he wanted to know. Then he took a proactive stance, following up with casual information-gathering conversations, even if it meant talking with the offender. When he witnessed mistreatment, he spoke up more often, even if he dreaded a negative reaction from the rude employee.

Within a few days Ivan recognized that he was logging fewer occasions of negative gossip and that he felt better about himself and his workplace: "I don't know whether anyone else would notice a difference—people already thought I was fair and supportive—but I know that I've changed. And there's another benefit for all of us. I'm seeing less incivility around me. I think speaking up when colleagues or subordinates are rude can really make a difference. It puts them on alert that somebody is watching and cares how everyone is treated."

ENLIST THE HELP OF TRUSTED COLLEAGUES

If coaches can focus acutely on your shortcomings and the changes you need to make to create a more civil you, so too can your peers. A first-rate example comes from one of our own workplaces. Business schools can be more uncivil than most outsiders might suspect. With professors facing tough standards for tenure, heavy teaching loads, and rising expectations from students, administrators, and boards of trustees, pressure can spill into uncivil words and deeds. Incivility in our world often flares up during presentations, when overly zealous professors vigorously interrogate visiting professors in an effort to prove their own superior intellects. At one of our schools we apply sports know-how to take the edge off these encounters and to help our colleagues avoid tripping over their own abrasiveness.

We warn colleagues of their potentially offensive behavior by using subtle hand signals to indicate the equivalent of soccer's yellow and red cards. The yellow card hand sign is a solid warning, letting the interrogator know that he needs to think about the way he's phrasing his questions, the tone he's adopting, and the intensity of his follow-up comments and questions. The red card signal means he's done for the session; in his colleague's view, he's been so offensive (repeatedly, and after fair warning) that he's being ejected from the "game." At the red card signal, fellow faculty members have learned to button it (and to keep their mouths shut!)—no more, not today.

The system works very well. It keeps us all watching for incivility, in others and in ourselves, before there are flare-ups that could spin out of control. Would-be offenders catch the hand signals quickly because they're aware of the system and want to curtail their incivility before they become offenders. Presenters benefit too. They have told us how collegial our group is and how friendly we are to outsiders. We suspect that our organization also benefits; since the presenters are treated civilly and feel comfortable working with our group, they see (and then describe) our environment in the best light. The exceptional value of the yellow/red card approach is that it catches offenders in the act—it identifies the uncivil behavior as it occurs—and it provides discreet feedback immediately.

The nature of behavioral changes that you may choose as you evaluate your ABCDs will vary according to your own style of uncivil behavior and your personal goals for improvement. Nonetheless, there are four essential behaviors that every offender should follow regardless of the context, the individuals involved, or mood at the time:

- **Listen fully.** This wide-ranging recommendation applies to many specifics, like turning off your cell phone/e-mail/text-messaging during meetings as well as focusing on the speaker rather than daydreaming, searching the room visually for the person you *really* want to talk to, or just zoning out because that's easier.

- **Increase your sincere use of words that convey civility.** Remember "please" and "thank you." "Excuse me" also boosts civility, as does "I'm sorry." We recommend apologizing whenever you are so inclined—and even when you're not.

- **Take less credit, give more.** In the short term you'll come across as more civil; in the long term (remember, bad behavior *costs*), your generosity will build social credits.

- **Think before you speak.** Refrain from wisecracks or one-upmanship that might be embarrassing, hurtful, disrespectful, or demeaning. As executive guru-coach Marshall Goldsmith noted, "If you're silent, no one can know how you really feel, and perhaps you'll avoid making an ass of yourself."

  Thinking before you speak when *responding* has physiological merit too. It adds a buffer against amygdala hijacking. The hesitation while you're keeping your mouth shut gives your brain an extra moment when the amygdala kicks in. By hesitating, you let the neocortex do its thing before leaping on your amygdala's impulses to act. That brief lapse could curtail an impulsive, uncivil comment or response. Go for

  Experience —> *think* —> respond

  not

  Experience —> respond —> *regret*

17

What Could Society Do?

We need business to give practical meaning and reach to the values and principles that connect cultures and people everywhere.

—Ban Ki-Moon, secretary-general
of the United Nations

INCIVILITY IS NOT just a workplace issue, it is a societal issue. Happily, our communities are recognizing the power and importance of living in a civil environment, and specific initiatives are already under way at local, state, national, and global levels, all of which hold promise for enhancing civility.

However, civility is not something that can be approached or achieved in terms of a specific program or initiative. To become more civil, society and the individuals and institutions constituting it need to pay more attention to the quality of relationships. Society must be more aware of the way evolving technology and social conditions have transformed interpersonal connections. Most important, we all need to make sure we slow down and spend the time necessary to treat others around us with respect.

Small changes can have a huge impact on social phenomena. Criminologists, social scientists, and physicians have demonstrated that you can stop social and medical syndromes from spreading by containing contaminants before a tipping point is reached. In our research for this book, we discovered many grassroots efforts that are curbing incivilities locally before they reach endemic proportions. In programs like Civility Project (Cleveland Heights, Ohio), Because It Matters (Venice, Florida), Speak Your Peace (Duluth, Minnesota), and Choose Civility (Baltimore, Maryland), municipal governments are partnering with schools, public libraries, and local colleges to educate students and others about civility's benefits.[1] In Cleveland Heights, a civility coordinator has been hired to teach students character development, empathy, compassion, and conflict resolution. In Howard County (part of the Baltimore-Washington metro area), forty community partners, including the public school system and county library, have come together to promote civility through workshops, discussions, and book distributions. More than forty thousand citizens in the area proudly display the initiative's CHOOSE CIVILITY bumper stickers.[2]

A Missouri minister set out to change the world, one griper at a time. His challenge: Stop griping for twenty-one days straight. To keep yourself honest, you get a purple plastic "Complaint Free" bracelet with instructions to move your bracelet to the other hand if you catch yourself whining, complaining, or gossiping—in essence, being uncivil. Sound easy? Try it. It even took the good pastor multiple tries before he could achieve it. Nonetheless, the popularity of the concept has caught on; more than six million people around the world are making the effort.

Community efforts put the spotlight on civility, but psychiatrists like Robert Coles[3] believe that moral values, including civil behavior, take root during childhood through the modeling and lessons of parents and teachers. Americans seem to agree. In a recent national poll that revealed widespread discontent with incivility in American society, more than four out of five respondents blamed parents for rampant rudeness.[4] According to those polled, parents don't teach their kids respect, and they are poor role models when it comes to civility.

In light of this accusation, we are encouraged to find school and sports programs at all levels that foster and celebrate civility in children, their teachers, and parents. National programs like Operation Respect and Teachers and Students for School Civility promote respect, responsibility, and compassion at school. Businesses have stepped up too. The textbook publisher McGraw-Hill supplies conflict resolution videos and curricula free of charge to more than forty thousand participating teachers. Another program, Character Counts, draws together leading youth organizations (e.g., the YMCA, 4-H, Little League, Boys & Girls Clubs) and educational associations (e.g., the National Education Association and the National Association of Secondary School Principals) to encourage respect and build character. Their collaborative efforts culminate in National "Character Counts!" Week, a program endorsed annually by the U.S. president, both houses of Congress, and numerous governors and mayors. During the week, children participate in art and essay contests, parades, and other events that spotlight respect, responsibility, fairness, and caring, what we would call civility.[5]

At the university level, honor codes to reduce cheating have existed for centuries. More recently schools have been adapting their credos to instill interpersonal respect, thus fostering civility. Our own institutions have included phrases like "Emphasize positive human relationships" and "Honor all people." Classroom-based service learning programs are also cropping up in colleges as a hands-on mode of putting civility into practice. Professor Amy Kenworthy, who has received international recognition for her efforts in the United States and Australia, requires her business students to donate their time in elementary and high schools, where they lead programs to eliminate bullying by instilling respect and civility. Efforts are springing up in college athletics too. Member schools of the Atlantic Coast, Pacific Ten, and Southeastern conferences have eliminated the very profitable sale of alcohol at all their games because they believe that inebriation can lead to incivility and dangerous behavior. Similar alcohol bans at the California State University (CSU), America's largest public university system, were put in place to address "incidents of poor sportsmanship, disorderly conduct and a negative game atmosphere," behaviors we would deem uncivil.[6]

Many institutions demand civil behavior from their athletes, but some have gone a step further, adopting rules of civility for fans. In many towns, youth sports can be an amazingly uncivil arena, and the problem usually isn't the players. Sometimes it's the coaches; more often it's the parents. During practice, when things aren't going their way, some coaches verbally abuse their players, while others preach unsportsmanlike conduct, like targeting attacks on rivals who have been injured. During games, when things aren't going their way, some parents attack coaches, referees, opposing players, parents of opposing players, and one another. Many communities are trying to rein in such behaviors through civility codes and behavioral guidelines.[7] Florida's Jupiter-Tequesta Athletic Association requires parents to take an online course on how to behave before they can attend their children's athletic events.[8] In collaboration with the Catholic youth program Play Like a Champion Today, Notre Dame delivers workshops to help participating coaches and parents train others back home how to play and observe sports civilly.[9] Throughout the United States, the National Alliance for Youth Sports (NAYS) provides guidance to communities seeking to curtail "negative behavior plaguing youth sports programs across the country." In some limited cases, silent matches have even been mandated by local leagues. Officials of the Northern Ohio Girls Soccer League were so tired of incivilities from the sidelines that they held Silent Sunday games, banning thousands of parents and coaches from making any noise whatsoever during games. As an NAYS expert noted, it was a wake-up call, a "giant timeout for adults," and the athletes loved it.[10] In a similar mode at the college level, the Big Ten Conference uses a three-strike system to assure civility among fervent student fans. The first time the student section trespasses the rules, the school is warned privately, the second time it is warned publicly, and with the third warning, the school must disband the student section.[11]

Professional sports teams and stadiums are also adding policies and equipment to foster civility and maintain crowd safety. Uncivil behavior at Philadelphia Eagles games got so out of hand that officials set up an on-site court and jail at the team's stadium. The effects yielded only moderate improvement, but when the Eagles moved to a new stadium, they planned ahead and added high-tech equipment. The hundred new security cameras focused on players and fans have drastically reduced the incivilities of the past.[12]

New York has made it illegal throughout the state to interfere with professional sports events. Fans are prosecuted and jailed for uncivil offenses that get out of control. New York Mets vice president Robert Kasdon blamed previous escalation of incivility on weak repercussions: "Rowdy fans were simply escorted out of the stadium and released, which was akin to a traffic summons." Now, with the possibility of jail time, bad behavior has declined. "It's the most effective law of its kind," according to Kasdon. "Baseball is a family event, and this law helps us maintain that atmosphere."[13]

Efforts and initiatives to assure civility are appearing within professional circles. In journalism, reporters are investing time, print, and e-space to discuss and derail "incivility creep." In the wake of e-leveraged death threats to blogger Kathy Sierra, Internet icons like Tim O'Reilly have drafted codes of conduct for the blogosphere. In the practice of law, nearly half the state bar associations have created and adopted mandatory civility guidelines. Some lawyers and judges with whom we work even speculate that a program for civility and professionalism may be mandated soon by the U.S. Supreme Court.

As you'll notice, business has not played a dominant role in most of the local and national programs we've discussed so far. Although business is involved in some of these campaigns, we believe that its role is most viable and essential at the global level. The United Nations (UN) has operated at the nation-state level since its founding (1945), but in 2000 it initiated an unprecedented partnership to involve business in achieving humanitarian rights worldwide. As a UN publication notes, "The roles and responsibilities of business as a global force are becoming more urgent and complex, and concepts related to societal responsibility and sustainability are gaining recognition as essential elements in business management."[14] A new partnership, the UN Global Compact (UNGC), has already become the world's largest voluntary corporate citizenship initiative. More than thirty-five hundred businesses and more than a thousand nonbusiness partners (e.g., governments, business schools, civic associations) are collaborating in more than 110 countries to advance human rights, better labor conditions, environmental management, and corruption control.

Global Compact takes a two-pronged approach to business and human rights, demonstrating (1) how these elements are relevant for business worldwide and (2) what businesses can do to support the cause. Benefits to business associated with issues like risk management, expanded markets, and employee morale and retention are emphasized by the UNGC, but the compact also implores businesses to implement human rights initiatives simply because it is the right thing to do. As we understand the initiative, we believe that achieving workplace civility and respect could be a fundamental extension of the compact's goals. In a 2007 resolution, the UN encouraged further efforts by businesses to "take into account not only the economic and financial, but also the developmental, social, human rights, gender and environmental implications of their undertakings . . . bringing social values and responsibilities to bear. . . . "[15] We believe that this broad-based resolution could provide another entry point for addressing workplace civility globally.

As exciting as all these programs and initiatives are, we close this book with the observation that fostering civility requires more than just formal programs. It requires that we pay attention to the quality of our relationships on all levels. In this regard, we want to introduce briefly two additional intellectual frameworks with some relevance for civility. The first is the concept of connectivity. Scholars and journalists have in recent years examined the manifold ways in which we are connected. The circuitry of six degrees of separation has achieved pop culture status through John Guare's play and cinema adaptation of the same name as well as movies like *Crash* and *Babel* and TV series like *Lost* and *Six Degrees*. Our world's smallness in social terms, an idea originally tested by Harvard psychologist Stanley Milgram and his colleagues in the 1970s, has been updated to incorporate cyberspace by Columbia sociologist Duncan Watts in his book *Six Degrees: The Science of a Connected Age*. The results confirm that Internet-assisted relatedness is astounding: We can reach out and touch with amazing speed and accuracy. But what about the quality of those connections?

More than a decade ago, Harvard professor Robert Putnam lamented the fraying of communal connections nationwide in his influential book *Bowling Alone*.[16] Data confirm that we no longer join clubs or engage in civic organizations as we once did. But Columbia Law Professor Cynthia Estlund questions Putnam's conclusion. Rather than plunge into social decay and solitude, she claims, we are forming bonds at work that replace and in many ways improve the connections we once made through our social and civic memberships.[17] Our connectivity hasn't decayed; it has simply moved. We no longer come together through homogeneous voluntary affiliations whose members look, think and act as we do. Now "not quite voluntary" workplace forces draw us together. That connectivity introduces greater challenges, but it also yields more resilient and diverse social ties. We are fundamentally "in this together" at work despite our differences in age, race, gender, ethnic orientation, or life experiences. To keep our jobs, we have to get the work done. And to get work done, we have to collaborate with people whom we might not otherwise choose to associate with.

We join workplaces voluntarily, and we stay voluntarily; but our membership is constrained by norms and rules that allow for smooth cooperation, reciprocity, and interdependence. To make and sustain those social ties, we must cooperate, reciprocate, collaborate, and extend mutual respect. In short, we must behave civilly, for good behavior soothes the required repetitive contact of work. Estlund contends that we must constrain conflict in order to connect. We would add that we must also bar conflict from going underground or otherwise becoming invisible. For us, social practices of connectivity offer even further buffers against the costs of bad behavior, as regards not only work-based outcomes but our humanity and well-being. Connectivity also suggests an approach to increasing the amount of civility in our world. We all could profit by becoming more aware on a daily level of the complex and technology-mediated bonds that join us as well as the ways in which conflict so easily goes underground.

Beyond greater awareness of connectivity, extending civility requires another resource that seems to be in short supply: time. As we saw earlier in the book, many offenders commonly complain that they "don't have time to be nice." Sixty percent blamed their bad behavior on being "overloaded with work." A potential remedy for this dilemma emerges when we consider what some are calling a revolutionary framework for life: slowness.

The United States is arguably the fastest-paced country on earth. We lead the industrialized world in the number of hours that we put in at work, and we boast endlessly of doing more, better, faster. Some of us thrive on the adrenaline rush triggered in our brains when we face endless demands on our time and achieve frenzied feats. But with this furious acceleration, fast never stays fast enough, so we shift into faster and then faster still. According to our research, the final tally for such endless acceleration must reflect the costs of squelched connectivity and quashed civility. In pursuit of speed, our country has become a hotbed of rage, whether on the road, in the air, or in the office. If there's a quicker way to do it, we pursue it, from *The One Minute Manager* to *The One Minute Bedtime Stories*, the consequences be damned.

What's to be done? We are not suggesting returning to the preindustrial era. But it might pay to rein ourselves in a little. In researching this book, we happened upon the Slow Movement, a growing international grassroots program organized to help advocates put the brakes on their lives. Enthusiasts attune themselves to a slower pace and a deeper appreciation of food, art, travel, music, or education. The Slow Food submovement alone boasts magazines, Web sites, international workshops, and eighty thousand members in more than a hundred countries. We believe that limited application of slowness could greatly benefit civility. It is clear to us that time is crucial in forging meaningful connections and addressing what's important in relationships. When slowness takes hold, quality surpasses speed. If we could slow down, even just a little bit, misunderstandings and relationship mistakes would decrease. As an added benefit, people might actually take more pleasure in their workplaces, their work, and one another. As Ralph Waldo Emerson once remarked, "This time, like all times, is a very good one, if we but know what to do with it."

Enhancing civility by slowing down does not come without costs; time after all is a finite commodity. Yet even in the workplace, slowness may be achieved by targeting what Carl Honore (author of the book *In Praise of Slowness*) prescribes as *tempo giusto*—finding balance by allocating the right amount of time to the specific pursuit at hand. We are by no means suggesting that people adopt a slow approach to all facets of their lives or even the majority of their work tasks. Rather, we're reminding people that building and nurturing relationships require civility and that civility sometimes takes just a little extra time. In the long run, investing a little bit of time to foster better relationships can add up to great savings. And the effects are broader than that. Championing respect and caring in the workplace will certainly improve civility throughout society. So much can be accomplished as organizations large and small discover that it pays to be civil.

APPENDIX

Confucius, Plato, Montezuma, Lincoln, and Others Knew the Value of Civility

History is the witness that testifies to the passing of time; it il-
luminates reality, vitalizes memory, provides guidance in daily
life and brings us tidings of antiquity.

—Cicero (106–43 BCE)

SOME COMMENTATORS take a moral approach to civility. Looking back at history, they applaud respectful behavior as a social good that made civilization possible and everyday life in society more pleasant. Others draw a different lesson. Civil behavior took root, they argue, not simply because civility was good for society but because it also conferred a positive benefit to the person behaving considerately. We argue for the latter view. Offering a quick survey of the history of civility from ancient times to the present, we argue that specific reasons for treating others well may have shifted over time, but people have always behaved civilly because it was ultimately in their social or individual interest to do so—in other words, because it *paid* to be civil.

Concern with civility goes back thousands of years. The Buddha (c. 563–483 c. BCE), for instance, beckoned believers to behave civilly by pointing to the spiritual benefits they would realize just by thinking well of others: "Those who are free of resentful thoughts surely find peace."

On the contrary, he posited that those who behave uncivilly or even just feel angry toward others wind up thwarting themselves: "You will not be punished for your anger, you will be punished by your anger."[1] The Buddha's contemporary Confucius (K'ung Fu-tzu, 551–479 BCE) taught emerging leaders how to conduct their affairs strategically, with compassion and diplomacy. Like the Buddha, Confucius turned attention to managing anger, emphasizing the poor strategic consequences of acting on it: "When anger rises, think of the consequences"; "Before you embark on a journey of revenge, dig two graves." Confucius's humanistic and moralistic teachings extolled the value of social roles, consideration toward subordinates, and compassion. The foundation of moral conduct, he argued, was internalized respect, which was exemplified by Mandarin scholar-officials through personal integrity, wisdom, and benevolence. *The Analects* (a collection of Confucius's sayings and anecdotes compiled after his death) offered a Golden Rule of deportment: "What you do not want done to yourself, do not do to others."[2]

Moving west, we find that Socrates (c. 469–399 BCE) advocated self-development, arguing that individuals should "be as they wish to seem," a maxim that speaks to the definitive practice of civility. Socrates believed that evil was rooted in ignorance and contended that it was more damaging to the perpetrator than the victim. Socrates's successor, Plato (c. 428–347 BCE), was in agreement: "False words are not only evil in themselves; they infect the soul with evil."[3] Advocating for what we would think of as civil behavior, not merely on the basis of self-interest but also as a general good, Plato said: "Good actions give strength to ourselves and inspire good action in others," and Aristotle (384–322 BCE) noted that it was important to monitor and contain one's anger so that it does not lead to uncivil flare-ups: "All men can become angry, but to be angry with the right person and to the right degree and at the right time and for the right purpose and in the right way—that is not within everybody's power and is not easy."[4]

Continuing our survey of civility through history, we next stop in Europe during the fourteenth and fifteenth centuries. Europe had been devastated by famines, wars, peasant rebellions, and the bubonic plague. The coming of the Renaissance brought a revival of learning and technological and cultural progress. Moral fervor energized by fear of the end of the world was replaced by the pursuit of glory for oneself and one's patron. An ideal of the Renaissance was the man of letters, intellectually sophisticated and classically schooled, who behaved properly toward others so as to avert embarrassing or shaming himself. Members of the aristocracy and rising middle class learned about social customs and civil practices of chivalry and heroism by reading great literature, such as the tales of King Arthur, Lancelot, and Guinevere (England and France) and such epic poems as the *Chanson de Roland* (France) and *El Cantar de Mio Cid* (Spain). Even those who couldn't read aspired to civil conduct as they listened to troubadours spin colorful tales. The courts emerged as aristocratic social centers where civil behavior was played out and put on display.[5]

To be courtly was to be refined, and refinement was exemplified in civil behavior. Those who behaved civilly and denied their primal impulses were accepted, given protection, and allowed proximity to others, while those who violated norms of civility weren't. Codes of conduct called for using your *own* knife at the dinner table and for wiping your hands on the tablecloth rather than on your coat, as many people then did. To behave civilly, you spit on the floor rather than on the table, kept your dirty hands out of the common serving bowl, and refrained from urinating at the table. The civil ideal was personified in the chivalric knight, yet members of the royal courts and the rising merchant class also learned rules for graciousness and deference. Scholars spread lessons of civility throughout the more refined regions of Europe, praising composure and control. In 1385, Geoffrey Chaucer (1342–1400), a British courtier, published the *Canterbury Tales*, a collection of moralistic stories told in the vernacular to educate and entertain the court and the middle class about human triumphs and foibles.[6] Adventures of Chaucer's characters depicted how middle-class well-being and happiness were linked to participation in what Chaucer called "compaignyes," socially bonding groups, such as guilds. Happy people ate together, worked together, formed alliances, and provided one another social support. To survive in this world, you needed to behave respectfully toward others.

Christine de Pizan (1363–1434), a court poet and social critic, wrote about the challenges and opportunities inherent in keeping civil company even before Columbus set sail for America. In *The Book of Man's Integrity*, she captured the essence of civility and its Renaissance payoffs: "He will not injure anyone through bad advice or dishonest pretensions or by any sort of extortion and so will call him a just man, will follow him, admire him, and honor him." Speaking to leaders at court, Christine de Pizan argued that the powerful should accept added responsibility for their behavior while warning against bad behavior. As she saw it, personal power and good conduct went hand in hand: "It is worse for [powerful people] because more faith is placed in what they say, and since they are in a more important situation they are more able to deceive if they want to, and as they really have less reason to do so, pretense and deception are truly unworthy of them."[7]

Although Pizan's social commentary and civil guidance were originally intended for the French court, their popularity spread among other European royals. In Italy two courtiers, Niccolò Machiavelli (1469–1527) and Baldassare Castiglione (1478–1529), were gaining immortality for their own diverging behavioral handbooks. Machiavelli's name is generally associated with duplicity and ruthlessness, but his advice was originally directed toward the Medicis to help them avoid becoming pawns in the political strife then occurring among warring city-states. By the time of Machiavelli's most famous work, *The Prince* (1532), hundreds of books illustrating ideal, positive courtly behavior had been written. Machiavelli contributed by acknowledging and addressing the reality of the dark side of human behavior. Attuned to man's self-serving nature, Machiavelli counseled that leaders had but two options: to show civility toward their foes or to seek vengeance fully. As he wrote: "Men should either be treated generously or destroyed, because they take revenge for slight injuries—for heavy ones they cannot."[8]

Unlike Machiavelli, Castiglione counseled courtesy over ruthlessness, care over force. In his *Book of the Courtier* (1528), Castiglione contends that power is best achieved through graciousness: "[H]e who has great things must not be abject or mean in spirit, yet very modest in speech, showing less confidence in himself than he has, lest self-confidence lead to rashness." Practical advice and conversational form made *The Book of the Courtier* a favorite among the aristocracy, including Holy Roman Emperor Charles V. As regards specific behaviors of the ideal courtier, Castiglione asserts the importance of behaving respectfully in the following ways: "He will not be thoughtless in sometimes saying things that offend. . . . He will not be obstinate and disputatious, as some are who seem to delight in nothing but to be troublesome and disagreeable like flies, and who make a point of spitefully contradicting everyone without discrimination."[9]

During the sixteenth and seventeenth centuries, notions of civility came to reinforce social order and relationships even further. By averting the embarrassment of offensive, unmannerly, uncivil behavior, royals assured their station and protection. The fork was introduced at this time, not as an eating utensil but as a substitute for one's hands when lifting meat from a common plate. Class differences were attributed to the use of proper dialect in England and France. Pronunciation, intonation, and jargon betrayed the speaker's origin and carried robust social implications. In English literature, Shakespeare satirized courtly rhetoric in *Love's Labours Lost* and *As You Like It* (first performed in the late 1500s), while acknowledging the popular imitation of Italian manners in *Richard II* (written around 1595). Later Molière (1622–1673) lampooned class distinction, highlighting the abuse of language and pompous ritual in comedic plays, including *The Bourgeois Gentleman* and *The Doctor Despite Himself.*

By the middle of the sixteenth century, guidance in civil deportment was cascading downward toward common folk and outward toward the New World. In *Il Galateo* (1551–1555), Florentine man of letters Giovanni della Casa took up a cause of Aristotle's, imploring ordinary middle-class readers to stop spitting, yawning, and belching lest they reveal their base animal instincts. Meanwhile, as the conquistadors arrived to plunder the New World, they entered with introductory civilities. Montezuma II and Cortés exchanged gracious salutations, and Montezuma lavished Cortés with gold and flowers. Despite their initial shows of respect, other "civil" rituals encountered in the New World defied European standards, even though they exemplified gestures and norms of superior decency and deference among the Aztec natives. Europeans were horrified by the Aztec practice of cannibalizing their enemies. Those they killed were butchered and consumed with decorum, adhering to Aztec standards for civility. With each offering, Montezuma got a thigh, the priests drank the blood, and even the lower classes were remembered with their fair share of the bounty. They dined on the rib cage.[10]

We may look at practices such as this as clearly barbaric behavior. But was it? Who, historically, were barbarians? History offers a relativistic definition of barbarism—that is, the barbarian is any people whose norms of civility are unlike your own. Greeks regarded the Celts, Indians, and Romans as barbaric; Persians put the label on Greeks and Romans; Chinese applied it to Europeans; Irish bestowed the title on the English, who returned the favor; and Romans applied the nomenclature to Gauls and Huns. For our ancestors, civility served as a helpful means of distinguishing insiders from outsiders and thus of safeguarding territory.

Moving ahead to the founding of the United States, we discover that George Washington (1732–1799) was an early advocate of civility. Before the American Revolution, Washington transcribed more than a hundred social rules based on the monastic guidelines published by a French Jesuit in 1595.[11] That advice, noted by Washington when he was only a teenager, is perhaps best generalized in the following statement: "Every action done in company ought to be with some sign of respect to those that are present." Washington's own recommendations included honesty and avoidance of cursing and swearing, the latter of which he proclaimed to be a "foolish and wicked practice." Two other Founding Fathers, Thomas Jefferson (1743–1826) and Benjamin Franklin (1706–1790), understood that diplomacy driven by strategic purpose was valuable in maintaining positive public opinion and goodwill. For them, civility was critical as a practical means to furthering one's self-interest. Ever mindful of potential detractors, Franklin recommended respectful encounters at all times, even when one was otherwise inclined: "Remember not only to say the right things in the right place, but far more difficult still, to leave unsaid the wrong thing at the tempting moment."

A similar dictum surfaced a century later. This time the sage was Abraham Lincoln (1809–1865): "It is better to remain silent and be thought a fool than to open one's mouth and remove all doubt." Lincoln's appeal for civility in the face of adversity "with malice toward none" (from his second inaugural address, as the United States was being torn asunder) is also evident in his timeless maxims: "If you look for the bad in people expecting to find it, surely you will" and "I don't like that man. I must get to know him better."

As the Civil War ended, the promise of ascending into a more exclusive social milieu motivated a preoccupation with civility, etiquette, and manners among the middle class. Refinement was no longer dictated by birth; now those willing to study and emulate the behaviors of upper classes could achieve higher social standing. Guidelines for civility were decoded, circulated, and popularized in the United States through inexpensive etiquette manuals and magazines. Periodicals such as *Godey's Lady's Book*, *Harper's Bazaar*, *Home Magazine*, and *Vogue* lauded gentility as the product of self-denial and discipline, a quality accessible to anyone who could muster the will. During this era, poet-essayist-minister Ralph Waldo Emerson (1803–1882) was a proponent of personal integrity. His aphorisms affirm the benefits of civility: "Trust men and they will be true to you; treat them greatly and they will show themselves great"; "you cannot do a kindness too soon, for you never know how soon it will be too late."

With the twentieth century came mass production, consumerism, increased use of technology, greater visibility and power for women and minorities, and a growing reality of social fragmentation. As historian John Kasson points out in *Rudeness and Civility*, a single code of civil deportment was no longer practical, but interest in self-improvement and social success was on the rise.[12] There may be no greater expression of this interest than Dale Carnegie's *How to Win Friends and Influence People*, a self-help guide to building and maintaining personal connections.[13] Carnegie's steps toward optimizing business relationships and personal success were first published in 1936; the book remained on the *New York Times* best seller list for more than a decade. By behaving civilly, Carnegie argued, readers could build their networks and assert their power. Once again civil behavior was lauded on the basis of its efficacy—because *it paid back dividends* to the person who behaved well.

And that is our point. Although the social context for respectful behavior has changed, an abiding sense of its utilitarian purpose has not. Civility has always been directed at securing and surpassing one's social station, whether this meant a better way of life while dining at a common table, surviving as a player in the royal court, or rising from middle class to upper middle class. Those who want to get ahead have learned to do things like control bodily functions, eat with utensils, use appropriate language, and be mindful of others; those who didn't do these things paid the price for bad behavior. As we've shown in this book, it's no different today.

Rude Awakenings

- Preoccupation with civility has a long history.
- Throughout history, philosophers and other commentators have reflected on the positive benefits that accrue to a person who behaves respectfully toward others.
- Modern manners developed through the attempts of courtiers, nobles, and others to gain position through civility.
- America's Founding Fathers lauded respectful behavior as serving one's own self-interest.

ACKNOWLEDGMENTS

The insights here were brought to life by thousands of individiuals who described their work experiences to us. We are grateful for their candor, which has educated and inspired us for more than a decade. Without their participation, this book would not exist.

We thank the companies that opened their doors to us so that we and our readers could benefit. In particular, we are grateful to Carla Christofferson, Jeff McHenry, Jason Passe, and Bill Shannon for facilitating entry into your firms.

We appreciate the keen eye and guiding hand of Lorin Rees, who saw the makings of a book in a brief article about our work. Thanks for your unwavering encouragement from the very beginning and for leading us to Seth Schulman, a gifted editor whose suggestions consistently added zest to our ideas.

We thank Adrienne Schultz and Adrian Zackheim, our editors at Portfolio, for lending their top-notch expertise about our audience and doing so with the utmost professionalism. Our thanks go as well to Brooke Carey and Courtney Nobile for the energy and creative ideas they have shared with us, and to Pearl Hanig for the best copyediting we have encountered.

We are, of course, appreciative of the many collaborative opportunities we have shared with academic colleagues whose efforts have informed our understanding of workplace incivility. In particular, Lynne Andersson, Judith Wegner, Amir Erez, Valerie Folkes, and Deborah MacInnis, thanks for your acumen and kindness. Your work helped shape this book. Working with each of you opens our eyes and lifts our spirits. Thanks to John Boudreau, Mark Kennedy, and Morgan McCall for your helpful advice and assistance. Also, we must single out Warren Bennis and Ed Lawler, whose wisdom will always set the bar for us.

We are incredibly grateful to our families and close friends for their support. We appreciate your enthusiasm about the practical importance of our work and your willingness to make our raw ideas top priority when requested. To family members Jim Pearson, Carrie Porath, Tripp Cherry, and Sarah Porath, thanks for sharing personal experiences and thoughtful recommendations.

Finally, our deepest thanks go to Bryan and John Pearson, Jim Marine, Michael, Mark, Kathleen, and Neil Porath for your kind and generous spirits. We have valued every idea, resource, word of encouragement, and critique that you have shared with us, as you will recognize throughout this book.

NOTES

_____

Foreword: Little Murders

1. Stephen Smith. "Heart Attack, Eh? Boss May Be Cause," *Boston Globe*, November 25, 2008.
2. Juan Jose Cruz. "One of Those Little Things You Learn to Live With," *Americana*, Spring, 2003.

The Cost of Workplace Incivility

1. W. Cascio, and J. Boudreau. *Investing in People: Financial Impact of Human Resource Initiatives*. New Jersey: FT Press, 2008.
2. M. P. Leiter and C. Maslach. *Banishing Burnout*. San Francisco: Jossey-Bass, 2005.
3. J. Connelly. "Have We Become Mad Dogs in the Office?" *Fortune* 130, no. 11 (1994):197–99.

Introduction

1. M. P. Leiter and C. Maslach. *Banishing Burnout*. San Francisco: Jossey-Bass, 2005.

Chapter 1: What Is Incivility?

1. L. M. Andersson and C. M. Pearson. "Tit for Tat? The Spiraling Effect of Incivility in the Workplace," *Academy of Management Review* 24 (1999):52–71.
2. Admiral Rickover, interviewed by Diane Sawyer. *60 Minutes*. CBS News.

3. C. M. Pearson, L. Andersson, and C. L. Porath. "Assessing and Attacking Workplace Incivility," *Organizational Dynamics* 29 (2000):123–37.
C. M. Pearson and C. L. Porath. 2005. "On the Nature, Consequences and Remedies of Incivility: No Time for 'Nice'? Think Again." *Academy of Management Executive* 19 (2005):7–18.
4. "Out at Home Depot," *Toronto Star*, January 15, 2007.
5. B. Grow. "Out at Home Depot," *BusinessWeek,* January 4, 2007.
6. S. Mufson. "Exxon Mobil Shareholders Defy Board," *Washington Post*, June 1, 2006.
7. "NorthStar Takes on Exxon Mobil's CEO Pay Practices," http://www.northstarasset.com/newsletters/2Q06.htm.
8. R. F. Snow. 1979. "Charles Chapin," *American Heritage Magazine* 31, no. 1 (1979):30.

Chapter 2: How Prevalent is Incivility in Society, Really?

1. B. Cook. "When Youth Baseball Goes Really Bad: Pony League Coaches Did Unthinkable—Setting Up a Cancer Victim to Fail," MSNBC.com, August 11, 2006.
G. Garber. "Youth Team Pays High Price in Win-at-All Costs Game." ESPN.com, August 15, 2006.
R. Reilly. "You Make the Call: Is It Good Baseball Strategy or a Weak Attempt to Win?" Sports Illustrated.com, August 8, 2006.
2. D. L. Espelage; K. Bosworth; and T. R. Simon. "Examining the Social Context of Bullying Behaviors in Early Adolescence," *Journal of Counseling and Development*, 78, no. 3 (2000):326–33.
3. *Operation Respect*. DVD produced by Discovery Channel, 2004 (used in Operation Respect programs).
4. A. Barber. "Rough Language Plagues Schools, Educators Say," *USA Today*, March 11, 1997.
5. C. L. Porath; D. J. MacInnis; and V. S. Folkes. "Witnessing Incivility Among Employees: Effects on Consumer Anger, Global Judgments, and Repatronage." (Revised and Resubmitted to *Journal of Consumer Research*)
6. Ibid.
7. C. Palmeri and K. Epstein. "Fear and Loathing at the Airport," *BusinessWeek*, September 10, 2007.
8. J. Levere. "Flying in a Snit," *New York Times*, January 24, 2006.
9. M. Albom. "Airport Turmoil: A Real Pain in the Neck," *Los Angeles Business Journal*, April 16, 2001.

10. J. Sharkey. "Right There on the Tarmac, the Inmates Revolt," *New York Times*, August 14, 2007.

11. G. Zumwalt. "The Staff of Life." Oklahoma Board of Medical Licensure and Supervision, January 2003.

12. A. Schneider. "Insubordination and Intimidation Signal the End of Decorum in Many Classrooms." *Chronicle of Higher Education*, 1998, http://chronicle.com/colloquy/98/rude/background.htm.

13. Ibid.

14. "Bachelet Says Chilean U20 Players Unjustly Treated by Toronto Police," *International Herald Tribune*. July 20, 2007.

15. B. Saporito. "Why Fans and Players Are Playing So Rough," *Time*, December 17, 2004.

16. "Honduras Snaps U.S. Home Unbeaten Streak," CNNSI.com, September 1, 2001

17. W. Nack and L. Munson. "Out of Control," *Sports Illustrated*, July 24, 2000.

18. W. E. Warnock. "Good Intentions Should Trump Bad Feelings," *Chapel Hill News*, October 21, 2007.

Chapter 3: What Could Incivility Cost a Company? A Case Study

1. For estimations and examples, see W. Cascio and J. Boudreau. *Investing in People: Financial Impact of Human Resource Initiatives.* New Jersey: FT Press, 2008.

2. J. K. Harter, F. L. Schmidt, and T. L. Hayes. "Business Unit-Level Relationships Between Employee Satisfaction, Employee Engagement, and Business Outcomes: A Meta-analysis," *Journal of Applied Psychology* 87 (2002):268–79.

3. For details that may help you compute these and other costs, see Cascio and Boudreau.

4. The company assumed that targets left earlier or started later by fifteen minutes total per week for the year.

5. The company decided to invest in EAP because of incivility, which cost $1 million (10,000 employees × approximately $100/year). It added an estimated $500,000 of miscellaneous stress/health care costs.

6. 5000 episodes × 10% that report it to HR × 15 hours managing it × $35/hour (the cost of the time of its average HR employee).

Chapter 4: The Roots of Workplace Incivility

1. L. Truss. *Talk to the Hand*. New York: Gotham Books. 2005.
   P.M. Formi. *The Civility Solution*. New York: St. Martin's, 2002.
2. S. L. Carter. *Civility*. New York: Basic Books, 1998.
3. http://www.upenn.edu/almanac/volumes/v53/n32/civility.html.
4. Carter, *Civility*.
5. R. Remington and M. Darden. *Aggravating Circumstances: A Status Report on Rudeness in America*. New York: Public Agenda, 2002.
6. J. O'Toole and E. E. Lawler III. *The New American Workplace*. New York: Palgrave Macmillan, 2006.
7. Ibid.
8. Ibid.
9. Ibid.
10. S. Barley and G. Kunda. *Gurus, Hired Guns and Warm Bodies: Itinerant Experts in a Knowledge Economy*. Princeton, N.J.: Princeton University Press, 2004.
11. J. Zaslow. "The Most Praised Generation Goes to Work," *Wall Street Journal on Line*. April 20, 2997.
12. Ibid.
13. O'Toole and Lawler. *New American Workplace*.
14. B. Saporito. "Why Fans and Players Are Playing So Rough." *Time*, December 17, 2004.

Chapter 5: What a Waste! How Incivility Wrecks Performance

1. J. K. Rilling, D. A. Gutman, T. R. Zeh, G. Pagnoni, G. S. Berns, and C. D. Kilts. "A Neural Basis for Social Cooperation," *Neuron* 35 (2002):395–405.
   A. G. Sanfey, J. K. Rilling, J. A. Aronson, L. E. Nystrom, and J. D. Cohen. "The Neural Basis of Economic Decision-making in the Ultimatum Game," *Science*, (2003):1755–58.
2. C. L. Porath and A. Erez. 2007. "Does Rudeness Matter? The Effects of Rude Behavior on Task Performance and Helpfulness," *Academy of Management Journal*, 50:1181–97.
   ———. "Overlooked but Not Untouched: How Incivility Reduces Onlookers' Performance on Routine and Creative Tasks," *Organizational Behavior and Human Decision Processes*. 2009.
3. Ibid.
4. J. Connelly. "Have We Become Mad Dogs in the Office?" *Fortune*, 130, no. 11 (1994):197–99.

Chapter 6: Amygdala Hijacking: How Our Brains Respond to Incivility

1. J. LeDoux. *The Emotional Brain: The Mysterious Underpinnings of Emotional Life*. New York: Simon & Schuster, 1996.
2. Ibid.
3. A. R. Damasio. "Time-locked Multiregional Retroactivation: A Systems-Level Proposal for the Neural Substrates of Recall and Recognition," *Cognition* 33 (1989):25–62.
———. *Descartes' Error: Emotion, Reason, and the Human Brain*. New York: Grosset/Putnam, 1994.
———. *The Feeling of What Happens: Body and Emotion in the Making of Consciousness*. New York: Harcourt Brace, 1999.
4. See L. W. Barsalou, P. M. Niedenthal, A. K. Barbey, and J. A. Ruppert. "Social Embodiment," *Psychology of Learning and Motivation* 43 (2003): 43–92.
5. E. M. Hallowell. *Worry*. New York: Random House, 1997.

Chapter 7: Stress and Burnout

1. K. Reivich and A. Shatte. *The Resilience Factor*. New York: Broadway Books, 2002.
2. Ibid.
3. M. P. Leiter and C. Maslach. *Banishing Burnout*. San Francisco: Jossey-Bass, 2005.
4. R. S. Lazarus and S. Folkman. *Stress, Appraisal, and Coping*. New York: Springer, 1984.
5. C. Mayhew, P. McCarthy, D. Chappell, M. Quinlan, M. Barker, and M. Sheehan. "Measuring the Extent of Impact from Occupational Violence and Bullying on Traumatized Workers," *Employee Responsibilities and Rights Journal* 16 (2004):117–34.
6. E. M. Hallowell. *Worry*. New York: Random House, 1997.
R. M. Sapolsky. *Why Zebras Don't Get Ulcers*, 3rd ed. New York: Owl Books, Henry Holt, 2004.
7. L. M. Cortina, V. J. Magley, J. H. Williams, and R. D. Langhout. "Incivility in the Workplace: Incidence and Impact," *Journal of Occupational Health Psychology* 6 (2001):64–80.
8. Mayhew et al. "Occupational Violence."
9. H. Leymann. "The Content and Development of Mobbing at Work," *European Journal of Work and Organizational Psychology* 5 (1996):251–76.

10. A. Caspi, K. Sugden, T. E. Moffitt, A. Taylor, I. W. Craig, H. Harrington, J. McClay, J. Mill, J. Martin, A. Braithwaite, and R. Poulton. "Influence of Life Stress on Depression: Moderation by a Polymorphism in the 5-HTT Gene." *Science* 301 (2003):386–89.

11. See M. Seligman. *Helplessness: On Depression, Development and Death.* San Francisco: W. H. Freeman, 1975.

    D. Hiroto. "Locus of Control and Learned Helplessness," *Journal of Experimental Psychology* (1974):102.

    ——— and M. Seligman. "Generality of Learned Helplessness in Man," *Journal of Personality and Social Psychology* (1974):31.

    L. Engberg, G. Hansen, R. Welker, and D. Thomas. "Acquisition of Key-Pecking via Autoshaping as a Function of Prior Experience: 'Learned Laziness?'" *Science* 178 (1973):1002.

Chapter 8: Teams Pay a Price

1. J. O'Toole and E. E. Lawler III. *The New American Workplace.* New York: Palgrave Macmillan, 2006.

2. C. L. Porath, G. Spreitzer, and C. Gibson. "Antecedents and Consequences of Thriving," Paper presented at Academy of Management, Anaheim, CA. August 2008.

3. A. Edmondson. "Psychological Safety and Learning Behavior in Work Teams," *Administrative Science Quarterly* 44 (1999):350–83.

   ———, R. Bohmer, and G. Pisano. "Speeding Up Team Learning." *Harvard Business Review* (2001):5–11.

4. W. Bennis and P. W. Biederman. *Organizing Genius.* Reading, Mass.: Addison-Wesley, 1997.

5. J. H. Gittell. *The Southwest Airlines Way: Using the Power of Relationships to Achieve High Performance.* New York: McGraw-Hill, 2003.

6. T. Lipps. "Einfuhlung, innere Nachahmungand Organempfindung" ["Original Idea of Emotional Contagion"] *Archiv für die gesante Psychologie* 1 (1903):465–519.

   J. L. Lakin, V. E. Jefferis, C. M. Cheng, and C. L. Chartrand. "The Chameleon Effects as Social Glue: Evidence for the Evolutionary Significance of Nonconscious Mimicry," *Journal of Nonverbal Behavior* 27 (2003):145–62.

   E. Hatfield, J. Cacioppo, and R. L. Rapson. "Primitive Emotional Contagion," In M. S. Clark, ed. *Emotion and Social Behavior: Review of Personality and Social Psychology* 14:151–77. Newbury Park, CA.: Sage, 1992.

————. *Emotional Contagion*. New York: Cambridge University Press, 1994.

D. J. Howard and C. Gengler. "Emotional Contagion Effects on Product Attitudes," *Journal of Consumer Research* 28 (2001):189–201.

7. P. Totterdell. "Catching Moods and Hitting Runs: Mood Linkage and Subjective Performance in Professional Sports Teams," *Journal of Applied Psychology* 85 (2000):848–59.

————, S. Kellet, K. Teuchmann, and R. B. Briner. "Evidence of Mood Linkage in Work Groups," *Journal of Personality and Social Psychology* 74 (2002):1504–15.

8. S. G. Barsade. "The Ripple Effect: Emotional Contagion and Its Influence on Group Behavior," *Administrative Science Quarterly* 47 (2002):644–76.

9. S. L. Robinson and A. M. O'Leary-Kelly. "Monkey See, Monkey Do: The Influence of Work Groups on the Antisocial Behavior of Employees," *Academy of Management Journal* 41 (1998):658–72.

Chapter 9: When Employees Leave

1. G. Colvin. "Catch a Rising Star," *Fortune,* January 30, 2006, http://money.cnn.com/magazines/fortune/fortune_archive/2006/02/06/8367928/index.htm.

2. http://whymetlife.com/downloads/MetLife_Benchmarking_Report.pdf.

3. C. Joinson. "Capturing Turnover Costs." *HR Magazine.* July 2000.

4. W. Cascio and J. Boudreau. *Investing in People: Financial Impact of Human Resource Initiatives.* New Jersey: FT Press, 2008.

5. Colvin. "Catch a Rising Star."

6. This loss was calculated using: (2 times a salary at $200,000 × 6 attorneys) + (2 times a salary of $100,000 × 2 paralegals).

7. E. E. Lawler. *Treat People Right! How Organizations and Individuals Can Propel Each Other into a Virtuous Spiral of Success.* San Francisco: Jossey-Bass, 2003.

8. We used two times a salary of a hundred thousand dollars for five employees as a starting figure. That total does not include any estimate of talent lost because of added difficulties of hiring the best. For useful tables on how to compute these costs, see W. F. Cascio. *Managing Human Resources: Productivity, Quality of Work Life, Profits,* 2nd ed. New York: McGraw-Hill, 1989.

Chapter 10: Misery Loves Company: The Cost to Your Reputation

1. B. I. Lev, C. Petrovits, and S. Radhakrishnan. "Is Doing Good Good for You? Yes, Charitable Contributions Enhance Revenue Growth," July 2006, http://ssrn.com/abstract=920502.
2. J. Pellet. "The Reputation Question." *Chief Executive* 213 (2008):45–46.
3. C. L. Porath, D. L. MacInnis, and V. S. Folkes. "Witnessing Employee Incivility in a Service Encounter: Effects on Consumer Behavior." Working paper, University of Southern California.
4. R. Remington and M. Darden. *Aggravating Circumstances: A Status Report on Rudeness in America*. New York: Public Agenda, 2002.
5. "Consumer Complaint Handling in America: An Update Study," Technical Assistance Research Program, White House Office of Consumer Affairs, Washington, D.C., 1986.
6. J. MacGregor. "Customer Service Champs," *BusinessWeek*. February 21, 2008.
7. N. Tucker. "Taking a Whack Against Comcast," *Washington Post*, October 18, 2007.
8. C. L. Porath, D. J. MacInnis, and V. S. Folkes. "Witnessing Incivility Among Employees: Effects on Consumer Anger, Global Judgments, and Repatronage." (Revised and resubmitted to *Journal of Consumer Research*.)
9. R. Beck, http://www.usatoday.com/money/economy/2007-12-21-405412 5678_x.htm.
10. M. J. de la Merced. "After Chief Holds a Chat, Sallie Mae Stock Plunges." *New York Times*, December 20, 2007.

Chapter 11: Time Wounds All Heels: Even Offenders Lose

1. S. Caminiti. "America's Most Successful Businesswoman: Linda Wachner, the CEO of Warnaco, Cut the Debt, Took the Company Public, and Boosted the Stock Price 75%. Any Wonder Her Holding Is Worth $72 Million?" *Fortune*, June 15, 1992.
2. L. Kaufman. "Questions of Style in Warnaco's Fall," *New York Times*, May 6, 2001. Other quotations in this paragraph are from the same source.
3. B. McManaman. "Coughlin's Changes Lift Giants," *Arizona Republic*, February 5, 2008.
4. M. McCall, Jr., and M. Lombardo. *Off the Track: Why and How Successful Executives Get Derailed*. Technical Report 21. Greensboro, N.C.: Center for Creative Leadership, 1983. A version of this also appeared in M. McCall, Jr.,

and M. Lombardo. "What Makes a Top Executive?" *Psychology Today* 17 no. 2 (1983):26–31.

5. M. W. McCall, Jr. *High Flyers: Developing the Next Generation of Leaders.* Boston: Harvard Business School Press, 1998.

6. D. Jones. "CEOs Say How You Treat a Waiter Can Predict a Lot About Character," *USA Today*, April 17, 2006, http://www.usatoday.com/money/ companies/management/2006-04-14-ceos-waiter-rule_x.htm.

7. Ibid.
   W. H. Swanson. *Swanson's Unwritten Rules of Management.* Waltham, Mass: Raytheon Company, 2005.

8. J. Wooden and S. Jamison. *Wooden on Leadership.* New York: McGraw-Hill, 2005.

9. W. Levinson, D. L. Roter, J. P. Mullooly, V. T. Dull, and R. M. Frankel. "Physician-Patient Communication: The Relationship with Malpractice Claims Among Primary Care Physicians and Surgeons," *Journal of the American Medical Association* 277 no. 7 (2002):553–59.
   N. Ambady, D. LaPlante, T. Nguyen, R. Rosenthal, N. Chaumeton, and W. Levinson. "Surgeons' Tone of Voice: A Clue to Malpractice History," *Surgery* 132 (2002):5–9.

10. B. Rice. "How Plaintiff's Lawyers Pick Their Targets," *Medical Economics* 77 (2000):94–102.

11. Levinson et al. "Physician-Patient Communication."

12. Ambady et al. "Surgeons' Tone of Voice."

13. M. Gladwell. *Blink: The Power of Thinking Without Thinking.* New York: Back Bay Books, 2005.

14. W. M. Stallings and R. E. Spencer. "Ratings of Instructors in Accountancy 101 from Videotape Clips." Research Report No. 265, Office of Instructional Resources: Measurement and Research Division, University of Illinois, 1967.

15. N. Ambady and R. Rosenthal. "Half a Minute: Predicting Teacher Evaluations from Thin Slices of Nonverbal Behavior and Physical Attractiveness," *Journal of Personality and Social Psychology* 64 no. 3 (1993):431–41.

Chapter 12: Success! How Five Organizations Have Set the Course

1. Quotations regarding Starbucks came from an interview with David Pace by John Boudreau, "Human Resource Strategic Excellence." Teleconference

series from the Center for Effective Organizations, University of Southern California, 2006.

2. R. Pelosi. "DaVita," *Health Executive*, November 1, 2004, http://www.healthexecutive.com/content/view/581/.

3. "Total Renal Care Announces New Company Name," Investor Relations-DaVita, June 5, 2000.

4. Pelosi. "DaVita."

5. Ibid.

6. J. Pfeffer and R. Sutton. *Hard Facts, Dangerous Half-Truths, and Total Nonsense: Profiting from Evidence-Based Management.* Boston: Harvard Business School Press, 2006.

————. "Act on Facts, Not Faith: How Management Can Follow Medicine's Lead and Rely on Evidence, Not Half-truths." *Stanford Social Innovation Review* Spring 2006:40–47.

Chapter 13: Top Ten Things a Firm Should Do to Create a Civil Workplace

1. J. Wooden and S. Jamison. *Wooden on Leadership.* New York: McGraw-Hill, 2005

————. *The Essential Wooden.* New York: McGraw-Hill, 2006.

2. J. A. Bargh, M. Chen, and L. Burrows. "Automaticity of Social Behavior: Direct Effects of Trait Construct and Stereotype Activation on Action," *Journal of Personality and Social Psychology* 71 (1996):230–44.

3. D. Meyer. *Setting the Table: The Transforming Power of Hospitality in Business.* New York: HarperCollins, 2007.

Chapter 14: What's a Leader to Do?

1. A. B. Goldberg and B. Ritter. "Costco CEO Finds Pro-Worker Means Profitability: High Wages, Employee Benefits Build Loyalty—and P.R. Ambassadors." August 2, 2006, http://abcnews.go.com/2020/Business/story?id=1362779.

2. J. M. O'Brien. "A Perfect Season." *Fortune*, February 1, 2008.

3. Ibid.

Chapter 15: What's a Target to Do?

1. L. M. Roberts, G. Spreitzer, J. Dutton, E. Heaphy, and B. Barker. "How to Play to Your Strengths," *Harvard Business Review*, January, 1–6, 2005.
2. R. I. Sutton. *The No Asshole Rule*. New York: Warner Business Books, 2007.

Chapter 17: What Could Society Do?

1. R. Marech. "Thanks for the Civility: Mannerly Campaign Spreads Nationwide." *Baltimore Sun*, November 1, 2007. Like a number of other initiatives around the country, the Choose Civility campaign was inspired by P. M. Forni's *Choosing Civility: The 25 Rules of Considerate Conduct* (New York: St. Martin's, 2002), which brought public attention to civility as a quality-of-life issue.
2. M. Otto. "The Hippest New Trend? Civility: Maryland Counties Have a Nice Streak: Just Look at Those 'Please Drive Gently' Stickers," *Washington Post* (and *Los Angeles Times*), April 29, 2008.
3. R. Coles. *The Moral Intelligence of Children*. New York: Random House, 1997.
4. R. Remington and M. Darden. *Aggravating Circumstances: A Status Report on Rudeness in America*. New York: Public Agenda, 2002.
5. See http://www.operationrespect.org and http://charactercounts.org, respectively, for these and other details.
6. S. Wieberg. "Colleges Are Reaching Their Limit on Alcohol." *USA Today*, November 16, 2005, http://www.usatoday.com/sports/college/2005-11-16-colleges-alcohol_x.htm.
7. W. Nack, L. Munson, and G. Dohrman. "Out of Control: The Rising Tide of Violence and Verbal Abuse by Adults at Youth Sports Events Reached Its Terrible Peak This Month When One Hockey Father Killed Another," *Sports Illustrated*, July 24.
8. D. O. Relin. "Who's Killing Kids' Sports?" *Parade Magazine*, August 7, 2005.
9. K. Sheehan. "Conference Aims to Transform Culture of Youth Sports." University of Notre Dame, College of Arts and Letters, News and Stories, June 18, 2007. http://al.nd.edu/about-arts-and-letters/news/conference-aims-to-transform-culture-of-youth-sports/.
10. "Kids Have a Ball on 'Silent Sunday.'" ESPN.com, October 4, http://espn.go.com/soccer/news/1999/1003/95932.html.
11. E. Brady. "How Free Should Speech Be at Campus Games? Legal Rights and Civility Clash at Sporting Events." *USA Today*, February 6, 2004, http://www.usatoday.com/educate/college/education/articles/20040215.htm.

12. B. Saparito. "Why Fans and Players Are Playing So Rough." *Time*, December 17, 2004, http://www.time.com/time/magazine/artile/0,9171,1009619,00.html.

13. W. Hu. "New York Leads Politeness Trend? Get Outta Here!" *New York Times*, April 16, 2006.

14. "The Principles for Responsible Management Education." Published by UN Global Compact, July 2007, http://www.aacsb.edu/Resource_Centers/PRME_final.pdf.

15. Ibid.

16. R. D. Putnam. *Bowling Alone: The Collapse and Revival of the American Community*. New York: Simon & Schuster, 2001.

17. C. Estlund. *Working Together: How Workplace Bonds Strengthen a Diverse Democracy*. New York: Oxford University Press, 2003.

Appendix: Confucius, Plato, Montezuma, Lincoln, and Others Knew the Value of Civility

1. F. S. Mead, ed. 2001. *A Treasury of Spiritual Insights and Practical Wisdom*. Darien, CT: Federal Street Press,

2. Confucius. *The Analects*. Tr. D. C. Lau. London: Penguin, 1979.

3. Plato. *Five Dialogues*. Tr. G. M. A. Grube. Indianapolis, IN: Hackett Publishing Co., 2002.

4. Aristotle. *The Complete Works of Aristotle*. Ed. J. Barnes. Princeton, NJ: Princeton University Press, 1984.

5. N. F. Cantor. *The Civilization of the Middle Ages*. New York: Harper Perennial, 1993.

6. G. Chaucer. *Canterbury Tales*. Tr. N. Coghill. New York: Penguin, 2003.

7. C. C. Willard, ed. *The Writings of Christine de Pizan*. New York: Persea Books, 1994.

8. N. Machiavelli. *The Prince and Other Writings*. Tr. W. A. Rebhorn. New York: Barnes & Noble Books, 2003.

9. B. Castiglione. *The Book of the Courtier*. Tr. L. E. Opdycke. New York: Barnes & Noble Books, 2005.

10. M. Visser. *The Rituals of Dinner*. New York: Penguin, 1991.

11. R. Brookhiser. *Rules of Civility: 110 Precepts That Guided Our First President in War and Peace*. Charlottesville, VA: University of Virginia Press, 2003.

12. J. F. Kasson. *Rudeness and Civility*. New York: Hill and Wang, 1990.

13. D. Carnegie. *How to Win Friends and Influence People*. New York: Simon & Schuster, 1990.

FURTHER READING

Although we have included references to key publications throughout the text, we offer this list of our favorite books for those who want to read more about civility.

On civility

Forni, P. M. *Choosing Civility: The Twenty-five Rules of Considerate Conduct*. New York: St. Martin's Griffin, 2008.

Goldsmith, M. *What Got You Here Won't Get You There*. New York: Hyperion, 2007.

Sutton, R. I. *The No Asshole Rule*. New York: Warner Books, 2007.

Truss, L. *Talk to the Hand*. New York: Gotham Books, 2005.

When Good People Behave Badly: What Will You Do? Boston: Harvard Business School Press, 2004.

From historical/sociological/demographic perspectives

Caldwell, M. *A Short History of Rudeness: Manners, Morals and Misbehavior in Modern Science*. New York: St. Martin's Press, 1999.

Carter, S. L. *Civility: Manners, Morals, and the Etiquette of Democracy*. New York: Basic Books, 1998.

O'Toole, J., and E. E. Lawler. *The New American Workplace*. New York: Palgrave MacMillan, 2006.

On emotions and emotional intelligence

Goleman, D. *Working with Emotional Intelligence*. New York: Bantam Books, 2002.

————. *Social Intelligence: The New Science of Relationships*. New York: Bantam Dell, 2006.

Hallowell, E. M. *Worry: Hope and Help for a Common Condition*. New York: Random House, 1997.

LeDoux, J. *The Emotional Brain*. New York: Simon & Schuster, 1996.

On age and gender

Fletcher, J. K. *Disappearing Acts*. Cambridge, MA.: The MIT Press, 1999.

Tannen, D. *The Argument Culture: Stopping America's War of Words*. New York: Ballantine Books, 1999.

On stress and burnout

Hallowell, E. M. *Connect: 12 Vital Ties that Open Your Heart, Lengthen Your Life, and Deepen Your Soul*. New York: Pocket Books, 1999.

————. *CrazyBusy*. New York: Ballantine Books, 2007.

Leiter, M. P., and C. Maslach. *Banishing Burnout*. San Francisco: Jossey-Bass, 2005.

Sapolsky, R. M. *Why Zebras Don't Get Ulcers*, 3rd ed. New York: Owl Books, Henry Holt, 2004.

For children

Leaf, M. *How to Behave and Why*. New York: Universe Publishing, 1946 (and 2002).

INDEX